# LEARNING
# FRENCH *from* SPANISH
### AND
# SPANISH *from* FRENCH

# LEARNING
# FRENCH *from* SPANISH
## AND
# SPANISH *from* FRENCH

## A SHORT GUIDE

*Patricia V. Lunn and Anita Jon Alkhas*

GEORGETOWN UNIVERSITY PRESS
WASHINGTON, DC

The publisher does not assume any responsibility for third-party websites or their content. URL links were active at time of publication.

Library of Congress Cataloging-in-Publication Data

Names: Lunn, Patricia V. (Patricia Vining), 1946- author. | Alkhas, Anita Jon, author.
Title: Learning French from Spanish and Spanish from French : a short guide/Patricia V. Lunn and Anita Alkhas.
Description: Washington, DC : Georgetown University Press, 2017.
Identifiers: LCCN 2016035842 (print) | LCCN 2016058872 (ebook) | ISBN 9781626164253 (pb : alk. paper) | ISBN 9781626164550 (hardcover) | ISBN 9781626164260 (eb)
Subjects: LCSH: Language transfer (Language learning) | Similarity (Language learning) | French language—Study and teaching. | Spanish language—Study and teaching. | Language and languages—Study and teaching.
Classification: LCC P118.25 .L86 2017 (print) | LCC P118.25 (ebook) | DDC 448.2/421—dc23
LC record available at https://lccn.loc.gov/2016035842

♾ This book is printed on acid-free paper meeting the requirements of the American National Standard for Permanence in Paper for Printed Library Materials.

18 17      9 8 7 6 5 4 3 2   First printing

Printed in the United States of America

Cover design by Martha Madrid.
Text design by click! Publishing Services.

# TABLE OF CONTENTS

## Chapter 1

¿Cómo se escriben los sonidos?/Comment s'écrivent les sons?

## Chapter 2

## Chapter 3

# PREFACE

*Learning French from Spanish and Spanish from French* is designed for adults who have already learned a language other than their native language. These learners have a special set of characteristics. First of all, they're used to thinking consciously about language, which can allow them to use what they know about one language to learn another. Also, and maybe even more importantly, they know about themselves as language learners. They find the process of language learning to be interesting in and of itself. And they know that even if they cannot become fully functioning native speakers of their next language, any degree of knowledge of a language can be interesting and useful.

A manual written for next language learners, then, has limited—but not trivial—goals. It should point out important details and provide good examples of those details. And, by explaining what to pay attention to and providing opportunities for observation, it should serve as a foundation for future learning. Much of this future learning will involve contact with the new language, and this contact will reveal details that have been intentionally excluded here.

All languages have some things in common, but certain languages—because of their shared history—have a great deal in common. This book will help speakers of one of a pair of related languages, Spanish and French, to capitalize on how the language they know is like the language they want to learn and to become aware of how the two languages are different.

# ABOUT THIS BOOK

This book is written for a very specific audience: people who have a working knowledge of either French or Spanish and want to learn the other language. You don't have to be totally fluent in one of the languages in order to use this book, but you do need to have reached the intermediate level in one language in order to be able to make comparisons. Then, as you work on your next language, you will also be able to gain insight into the language you already know.

The chapters that follow describe how Spanish and French are alike and how they differ. To write this description in the form of a manual—rather than an encyclopedia—it was necessary to leave out a lot. Hundreds of millions of people speak these languages on several continents, and there is considerable variation from one place to another. There is also variation based on the age, social class, education, and gender of speakers. With a few necessary exceptions, we have ignored this variation and talk only about two standard varieties: Latin American Spanish and European French. There may be places in the text—particularly in the chapter on pronunciation—where you say to yourself, "I know people who don't say it that way." That could be, but you can move beyond this manual to learn the idiosyncrasies of any specific variety of French or Spanish. The next section, Beyond This Book, contains many suggestions for continuing the process of learning your next language.

This book contains a lot of information and is designed to help you keep track of it. In all of the chapters, Spanish and French words are highlighted in red and blue, respectively. Where you see the icon 🔊 you can hear the words pronounced in audio files on the Georgetown University Press website. There are also simple exercises that allow you to check your understanding of the material. At the end of each chapter, there are suggestions for further practice. At the end of the book, you will find additional information:

- Parallel texts. These three short texts—a traditional tale, a news report, and an interview—are presented in parallel format in the two languages and allow you to see how some of the grammatical features of French and Spanish are used in context.
- Answer keys. The answers to the chapter exercises are found here.
- Spanish and French verb charts. Verb charts show the main patterns of conjugation.
- Glossary. A glossary provides definitions of terminology that is CAPITALIZED in the text.

Mastering a new language is a long-term endeavor. Since there are so many aspects of language to master, it is helpful to clarify your primary goals and the contexts in which you will most likely use the new language. In this way, you will be able to focus your efforts and make faster progress. The momentum created by such a targeted approach will motivate you to pursue your studies and ultimately to broaden your goals.

The parallel texts provided at the end of this book are a useful step toward the goal of interpreting written language with ease. The specific contexts in which you plan to use your next language may include keeping up with current events, watching television and films, pursuing a hobby, reading for pleasure, or conducting research. Once you have worked through the parallel texts provided, seek out other parallel texts that match your specific goals. In the early stages of your reading practice, we recommend professionally edited or translated texts. A news article from an online publication, for example, is a more reliable resource for standard, error-free language than a blog or the comment section following an online post (though these are a rich source of informal language use).

There are a few online newspapers that publish bilingual articles. These include *Le Courrier d'Espagne* (lecourrier.es), which offers a Spanish edition (lecourrier.es/category/version_espanola/); Reporters Without Borders, which is published in six languages including French and Spanish (en.rsf.org); and the French monthly *Le Monde Diplomatique*, which offers print and online editions in a number of Spanish-speaking countries, including Spain (www.monde-diplomatique.es) and Chile (www.lemondediplomatique.cl). You can also simply use a search engine to find and compare articles on a specific topic in both languages; because the articles you find may not be strictly parallel texts, this approach offers additional challenges that will strengthen your reading abilities.

There are other excellent resources for parallel texts. Many international organizations, nongovernmental organizations (NGOs), and multinational corporations have multilingual websites. Most publications of the United Nations and its agencies, for example, are available in all of its working languages, which include French and Spanish. Translations of classics, sacred texts, popular fiction, and nonfiction are widely available in print and online, and can be read side by side or sequentially in short segments. Free, open-content online sources like Wikipedia have multiple language editions. Look for other ways to incorporate regular reading practice into your schedule, such as by switching the language setting on your electronic devices, computer operating system, browser, and search engine (the search settings in Google, for example, offer the options of French and Peninsular or Latin American Spanish). Before tackling entirely unfamiliar texts, it can be highly motivating and effective to reread familiar texts that have been translated into your target language. Then, as you gain confidence and increase your reading abilities, you can begin reading without the support of parallel texts.

A similarly tiered approach is recommended as you learn to interpret spoken language in a variety of contexts, such as watching television, videos, and films, or listening to music, radio, podcasts, and conversations. The audio files that accompany this book, available on the Georgetown University Press website, will help you begin to train your ear. Reading a text while listening is an effective strategy for improving your listening comprehension, but you should avoid overreliance on written texts. We suggest that you make a practice of listening to the audio files regularly, alternating between simultaneous listening and reading, and listening without the text. This approach can be used with any text available in spoken and written form, and there are more and more options for finding such resources, ranging from audiobooks to films streamed online or on DVD with audio and subtitles in multiple languages. Specifically for learners of French and Spanish, there are online news services that can serve as transitional resources for developing interpretive skills in both reading and listening: Radio France Internationale regularly offers news segments in "easy" French on its website (www1.rfi.fr/lffr/statiques/accueil_apprendre.asp) and "News in Slow French" can be heard at www.newsinslowfrench.com. "News in Slow Spanish" is delivered daily by newscasters from Spain and Latin America (www.newsinslowspanish.com). Text-to-Speech (TTS) applications such as www.naturalreaders.com are now widely available and can convert written text into computer-generated speech with a range of voice options (e.g., male or female, French speaker from Canada or France, etc.). Open-source audio-editing programs such as Audacity make it possible to slow down speech samples without significant distortion. Ultimately, through frequent and judicious use of these tools, you will be able to build up your interpretive abilities and move toward comprehending increasingly complex language in a broad variety of contexts.

The time and effort you put into the interpretive skills of reading and listening will bear fruit as you practice interpersonal communication in spoken interactions, whether face-to-face or mediated by telephone or by videoconferencing, and in written interactions in e-mail exchanges, text messages, or chat rooms. As soon as possible, take advantage of opportunities for communicating with other speakers in the language. Language classes offer valuable guided practice in speaking and writing. Look for organizations in your community, such as Latino cultural centers or Alliance Française or Instituto Cervantes chapters, that offer language- and cultural-immersion activities and can help connect you to native speakers. There are, of course, many opportunities to practice speaking when traveling—even outside of the Francophone and Hispanophone worlds, since French and Spanish are popular languages of study in many countries. Participating in social-media platforms such as Facebook and Twitter, or playing online games that include a text-based chatting option, can provide valuable practice in interpersonal written communication with native speakers and other language learners. There are also an increasing number of online communities, such as LiveMocha and Busuu, that facilitate video- and text-based language exchanges with native speakers. These online communities also offer valuable support if your language goals include presenting information formally in speaking or writing, whether face-to-face or mediated (e.g., making a toast, performing in a play, writing a personal or business letter, delivering a paper at a conference).

Remember that the different modes of communication support one another. The more skillful you become as a reader and listener, the more vocabulary and structures you will have available to you when you speak or write. And, when speaking and writing, the challenges you encounter will alert you to the need for further study on a specific topic. To support your language use in all modes of communication, you will need reliable dictionaries and reference grammars in both languages. A French-Spanish bilingual print dictionary is an excellent investment (to find one to purchase online use the search terms "diccionario francés español" or "dictionnaire espagnol français"). There are also many excellent free online dictionaries, such as www.wordreference .com, that allow you to toggle between different language options, such as French-French, Spanish-French, English-Spanish, etc. Many of them are also pronouncing dictionaries, a useful supplement to the phonetic transcriptions in your print dictionary. To learn the pronunciation of proper nouns (which can be especially challenging), we recommend www.forvo.com, a growing online digital archive of native speakers of dozens of languages pronouncing words requested by nonnative speakers.

You will want to use both print and online resources, but we offer a word of caution in the use of online translators and blogs. They can be excellent resources, but are most useful to those who know enough to recognize which translations or comments are most accurate and appropriate. A good option is an online dictionary that shows examples of language in context drawn from a large corpus of professionally translated texts on the internet (e.g., www.linguee.com or bab.la).

# ACKNOWLEDGMENTS

This is a new kind of project, and many people helped us figure out how to do it. At Georgetown University Press, David Nicholls encouraged us to submit a proposal, and Clara Totten saw it through to the end. While searching for that elusive balance between what to include and what to leave out, we got invaluable advice from Priscilla Charrat, Lea Cicchiello, Larry Kuiper, Ernie Lunsford, Terrell Morgan, Valérie Saugera, Will Travers, and Gabrielle Verdier. Marvin Guire (Paris, France) and Laura Mendoza-Montáñez (Bogotá, Colombia) gave voice to the contrastive words and texts, and Larry Linvik of the Language Resource Center at the University of Wisconsin-Milwaukee recorded them.

# INTRODUCTION

French and Spanish are Romance languages, members of the family of languages that also includes Catalan, Italian, and Portuguese. These languages developed from the Latin spoken in the Roman Empire. As a result, they have a great deal in common—though it is not the case that speakers of one of these languages can automatically speak the others.

With varying degrees of success, the Roman Empire imposed its language on the lands it conquered. Even after the official fall of the Roman Empire (478 AD), Latin continued to be the language of education, religion, and administration in much of Europe. Regional varieties of the language were diverging, but educated speakers were able to understand and communicate with one another in Latin, at least in formal situations.

All languages change over time. Immigration and emigration lead to diversity in populations; contacts with other cultures make it necessary to borrow new words; patterns of pronunciation result in the loss of some sounds and the emergence of others. During the Middle Ages, the varieties of Latin spoken in the former Roman Empire became more and more different from one another, and the unifying belief that all varieties of Latin were mutually intelligible became outmoded. The formation of the Spanish and French nations was accompanied by a belief that the languages spoken in the new nations were unique. In the 1492 grammar of Castilian—the basis of modern Spanish—the author says that the book will be useful to speakers of French (among other languages) who wish to communicate with the new Spanish state. Since then, Spanish and French have continued to diverge, both because national language policies have codified the differences between them and because colonialism has spread them to different parts of the world.

What do French and Spanish have in common? Both languages have the parts of speech they inherited from Latin: nouns, verbs, adjectives, adverbs, prepositions, etc. Both have retained some of Latin's complex

MORPHOLOGY, meaning that many words have endings that convey important information. Most nouns have endings that show which of two classes—conventionally called masculine and feminine—they belong to, and they also have marking for singular and plural. Most adjectives have endings that reflect the gender (masculine or feminine) and number (singular or plural) of the nouns they modify. Verbs in both French and Spanish have endings that identify the subject of the verb, the timeframe of the verbal event, and several other kinds of information as well. And the languages share thousands and thousands of words inherited from Latin.

# Chapter 1

## ¿CÓMO SE ESCRIBEN LOS SONIDOS?
## COMMENT S'ÉCRIVENT LES SONS?

As with all languages, the pronunciation of French and Spanish varies geographically, from place to place, and socially, from speaker to speaker. Describing all of this variation would be very complicated; the discussion here is based on the "standard" pronunciation of Latin America and France. (You might think of this as the careful speech of newscasters.) The goal is to show how the spelling of words—ORTHOGRAPHY—corresponds to standard pronunciation, and regional differences are mentioned only as they relate to spelling.

Because pronunciation changes constantly while spelling changes very slowly, there is never a one-to-one correspondence between how a language is pronounced and how it is written. Languages vary, though, in how clearly their spelling represents their pronunciation. **Spanish and French are very different in this regard: Spanish orthography is quite straightforward, while French orthography is more complicated.**

### 1A. STRESS AND ACCENT MARKS

Comparar/Comparer
Observe the relationship between the symbol ´ and the underlined, stressed syllable. **In Spanish, a syllable with an accent mark is always stressed; in French, the final syllable is stressed, whether it is spelled with an accent mark or not.**

🔊 *separé* vs. *séparé*
*repartí* vs. *reparti*
*Lulú* vs. *Loulou*
*televisión* vs. *télévision*

The stressed syllable in a word (or phrase) is more prominent than the others. It takes more energy to produce these syllables, and this energy produces greater tension and volume. **Stress is CONTRASTIVE in Spanish; that is, the location of stress in a Spanish word is part of its meaning. So, the spelling of Spanish words shows which syllable is stressed.** Changing where a word is stressed can change its meaning; the following words, in which stress falls on the first, the second, or the third syllable, mean different things: *término (terme)/termino (je termine)/terminó (il a terminé)*.

### Detalles/Détails

In English, as in Spanish, stress can change meaning. Think of words like the nouns *conflict, import, progress,* and *rebel,* stressed on the first syllable, vs. the verbs *conflict, import, progress,* and *rebel,* stressed on the last syllable. There are no contrasts like this in French.

**You can always identify the stressed syllable in a Spanish word by looking at its spelling.** If there is an accent mark ´ over a vowel, then the syllable containing that vowel is stressed. Most words, however, do not carry accent marks; the stressed syllable in these words can be identified using other spelling cues.

### Cue #1

If a word is spelled with a final vowel or -*n* or –*s*, as most words are, the next-to-last syllable is stressed (unless the accent mark ´ indicates otherwise). This means that adding the plural endings -*n* and -*s* to words ending in a vowel does not change where stress falls.

🔊 *come* vs. *comen*     *(mange, mangent)*
*todo* vs. *todos*      *(tout, tous)*

está vs. están       *(est, sont)*
menú vs. menús       *(menu, menus)*

*Cue #2*
If a word is spelled with a final consonant other than *-n* or *-s*, the last syllable is stressed (unless the accent mark ´ indicates otherwise).

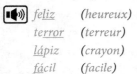

feliz      *(heureux)*
terror     *(terreur)*
lápiz      *(crayon)*
fácil      *(facile)*

Usually, the number of syllables in a word in Spanish is the same as the number of vowels. In some cases, though, there is more than one vowel in a syllable. The vowels *i* and *u* form DIPHTHONGS with adjacent vowels (i.e., the two vowels are in a single syllable). When *i* or *u* forms a syllable separate from an adjacent vowel, this is indicated with an accent mark (and is called *hiato* in Spanish).

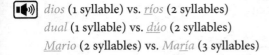

dios (1 syllable) vs. ríos (2 syllables)
dual (1 syllable) vs. dúo (2 syllables)
Mario (2 syllables) vs. María (3 syllables)

**1.1 Ejercicio/Exercice**

Identify the stressed syllable from the spelling of the word. The syllables appear in parentheses. Then listen to the audio.

Argelia      *(ar ge lia)*
Brasil       *(bra sil)*
Canadá       *(ca na da)*
Corea        *(co re a)*
España       *(es pa ña)*
Japón        *(ja pon)*
México       *(me xi co)*

| | |
|---|---|
| *Perú* | *(pe ru)* |
| *Turquía* | *(tur qui a)* |

**In French, stress is not contrastive, meaning that there are no words in French that are distinguished from others by stress alone,** like Spanish *término*/*termino*/*terminó*. Individual French words are consistently stressed on the last syllable. For this reason, many words borrowed into Spanish from French are stressed on the last syllable (*champán*, *champiñón*, *jardín*, *menú*), and Spanish words borrowed into French are pronounced this way, too (*macho*, *margarita*, *Martinez*, *tapas*). In practice, stress in French often operates within phrases rather than words, with stress falling at the end of phrases.

Given that individual words are all stressed on the last syllable, accent marks are not used in French to show where stress falls. They are used, rather, to signal how the vowel *e* is pronounced. The acute accent (*accent aigu*) ´ over the vowel *e* signals that it is pronounced as in Spanish *de* (tense and closed); the grave accent (*accent grave*) ` and the circumflex (*circonflexe*) ˆ over the vowel *e* signal that it is pronounced as in Spanish *del* (lax and open).

**1.2** Ejercicio/Exercice

Listen to how the names of the countries in the previous exercise are pronounced in French. Remember: the symbol ´ does not show where stress falls in French (because stress always falls on the last syllable) but shows how the letter *e* is pronounced.

| | |
|---|---|
| *Algérie* | *(Argelia)* |
| *Brésil* | *(Brasil)* |
| *Canada* | *(Canadá)* |
| *Corée* | *(Corea)* |
| *Espagne* | *(España)* |
| *Japon* | *(Japón)* |
| *Mexique* | *(México)* |

| | |
|---|---|
| *Pérou* | *(Perú)* |
| *Turquie* | *(Turquía)* |

 **1.3** Ejercicio/Exercice

Predict where the accent will fall on these words in French and Spanish. Then listen to see if your prediction was correct.

| | |
|---|---|
| *¡Bravo!* | *Bravo!* |
| *euro* | *euro* |
| *Félix* | *Félix* |
| *ferry* | *ferry* |
| *Lena* | *Léna* |
| *Romeo* | *Roméo* |
| *teléfono* | *téléphone* |

## Detalles/Détails

In Spanish, the symbol ´ is used in writing to distinguish one-syllable words from one another—for example, *mi (mon/ma)* vs. *mí (moi)*, *se (se)* vs. *sé (je sais)*, *si (si)* vs. *sí (oui)*, *tu (ton/ta)* vs. *tú (tu)*. Similarly, in French, the symbol ` is used in writing to distinguish *a (ha)* from *à (a)*, *la (la)* from *là (allá)*, and *ou (o)* from *où (donde)*; and ^ is used to distinguish *du (del)* from *dû (debido)* and *sur (sobre)* from *sûr (seguro)*. In both languages, the members of these pairs of words are pronounced exactly the same; the so-called accent marks are used for purely orthographic reasons.

## 1B. CONSONANTS

**Same sounds, different letters**
*Ñ and ll/gn and ll*
The palatal nasal is spelled *ñ* in Spanish, but *gn* in French.

 *araña ~ araignée*
*bañar ~ baigner*

*coñac* ~ *cognac*
*España* ~ *Espagne*

There was once a palatal lateral in Spanish that was spelled *ll*, but in most dialects this sound has merged with *y*. As a result, *ll* often sounds the same in French and Spanish.

*billete* ~ *billet*
*muralla* ~ *muraille*
*maravilla* ~ *merveille*
*vainilla* ~ *vanille*

In French, though, *ll* sounds like the consonant *y* only when preceded by the vowel *i* or a diphthong ending in *i*; otherwise, it just represents *l*, as in *folle*, *nulle*. The words *ville* and *mille*, whose spelling was changed to make the words more like their Latin roots, are two of a small number of exceptions. A single final *l* also sounds like the consonant *y* when preceded by a diphthong ending in *i*, as in *travail* and *détail*.

*F and t/ph and th*
In French, the DIGRAPHS (two letters representing one sound) *ph* and *th* represent the same sounds as *f* and *t*, respectively. In Spanish, *ph* and *th* are used only in the "fancy" spelling of proper names like *Raphael* and *Thiago*.

**Same letters, different sounds**
*B and v*
The letters *b* and *v* represent the same sound in Spanish (like French *b*, with a softer variant between vowels); speakers of Spanish often commit spelling errors because they don't know which letter to write. In French, these letters represent contrastive sounds.

Observe that the words in each pair below differ in Spanish only in spelling (i.e., they are homonyms), while in French they differ in both spelling and pronunciation.

| SPANISH | | FRENCH | |
|---------|--|--------|--|
| *basto* **vs.** *vasto* | *(grossier, vaste)* | *bain* **vs.** *vin* | *(baño, vino)* |
| *baya* **vs.** *vaya* | *(baie, aille)* | *boire* **vs.** *voir* | *(beber, ver)* |
| *bello* **vs.** *vello* | *(beau, poil)* | *bon* **vs.** *vont* | *(bueno, van)* |
| *tubo* **vs.** *tuvo* | *(tube, a eu/tenu)* | *habit* **vs.** *avis* | *(hábito, aviso)* |

In Spanish, the letters *b/v*, *d*, and *g* represent slightly different sounds depending on their position in a word or phrase. In absolute initial position (i.e., after silence) or after *n* or *m* (nasal consonants), they represent hard sounds (OCCLUSIVES). In the middle of words or phrases, and especially between vowels, they represent a softer variant of these consonants, made when the articulation is not completely closed (APPROXIMANTS). This variation does not occur in French. Each example below contains both the hard sound and the soft sound. Listen for the difference.

*bebé (bébé)*
*Vamos, por favor. (Allons-y, s'il vous plaît.)*
*un dedo (un doigt)*
*de nada (pas de quoi)*
*griego (grec)*
*Gabriel, no lo hagas. (Gabriel, ne le fais pas.)*

*C, s, and z*
In Latin American Spanish the letters *s* and *z*, and *c* before *e/i*, represent the same sound (which leads to misspellings, of course).

Observe that these pairs of words have the same pronunciation (i.e., they are homonyms) in Latin American Spanish.

*ves* **vs.** *vez (tu vois, fois)*
*casar* **vs.** *cazar (épouser, chasser)*
*rosa* **vs.** *roza (rose, il frotte)*
*sien* **vs.** *cien (tempe, cent)*
*sueco* **vs.** *zueco (suédois, sabot)*

In standard European Spanish the letters *c* before *e/i* and *z* are pronounced like the *th* in the English words *thin* or *tooth* (French does not have this sound). So, the paired words above are not homonyms in most of Spain. Listen to the same list pronounced in European Spanish.

*ves* vs. *vez*
*casar* vs. *cazar*
*rosa* vs. *roza*
*sien* vs. *cien*
*sueco* vs. *zueco*

 **1.4** Ejercicio/Exercice

Predict how the letters *c*, *s*, and *z* will be pronounced in European Spanish in these sentences from the beginning of *El pastor mentiroso*. Then listen to them.

> *Había una vez un joven pastor que tenía muchas ovejas. A veces el pastorcito se aburría de estar solo en el campo.*

In French, *s/c* and *z* represent two contrastive sounds. At the beginning of words, *s* and *c* before *e/i* represent one sound, and *z* another. Spanish has only the former.

 *celle/sel* vs. *zèle* (*la (que)/sal, celo*)
*cinq* vs. *zinc* (*cinco, zinc*)
*scène* vs. *zen* (*escena, zen*)

Within words, this contrast in French can be spelled several different ways. A double *s* between vowels is pronounced [s], but a single *s* is pronounced [z]. The *t* of the SUFFIX *-tion* (and, less predictably, of other suffixes beginning with *ti*) is also pronounced [s].

 *assure* vs. *azur* (*garantiza, azul*)
*face* vs. *phase* (*faz, fase*)

*douce* vs. *douze (dulce, doce)*
*russe* vs. *ruse (ruso, artimaña)*

## Ch

The sounds spelled *ch* are different in the two languages. In French, *ch* sounds like the *sh* of English *ship*. In Spanish, *ch* sounds like the *ch* of English *chip*. To spell this latter sound, French adds a *t* before the *ch*: *Tchad*.

 *chal ~ châle*
*charcutería ~ charcuterie*
*cheque ~ chèque*
*Chile ~ Chili*
*chocolate ~ chocolat*

In some words of Greek origin in French, *ch* represents [k]: *archéologie, chaos, chronologie, orchestre (arqueología, caos, cronología, orquesta)*.

## G and j

In both French and Spanish, the letter *j* and the letter *g* before the vowels *e* and *i* have the same pronunciation. In French, these letters represent a FRICATIVE sound made at the front of the palate, and in Spanish a fricative sound made at the back of the palate.

 *gente ~ gens*
*jirafa ~ girafe*
*jalea ~ gelée*
*jengibre ~ gingembre*

## R

Pronunciation of the letter *r* is very different in the two languages. In French, this consonant is pronounced with the **back** of the tongue, as a fricative or a trill, depending on dialect. In Spanish, it is pronounced with the **front** of the tongue as a trill when spelled double (*rr*) and at the beginning of words, and otherwise as a tap.

*correr ~ courir*
*Roberto ~ Robert*
*raro ~ rare*
*arribar ~ arriver*

 **1.5** Ejercicio/Exercice

The trilled *r* in Spanish can also be pronounced as a fricative; but, however it is pronounced, it contrasts with the single *r* between vowels. The single *r* is a tap with the front of the tongue, like the *dd* or *tt* of English *ladder* or *latter*. Listen to these words and then imitate the pronunciation.

| | |
|---|---|
| *cerro* **vs.** *cero* | *(colline, zéro)* |
| *corro* **vs.** *coro* | *(je cours, chorale)* |
| *mirra* **vs.** *mira* | *(myrrhe, regarde)* |
| *parra* **vs.** *para* | *(treille, pour)* |
| *perro* **vs.** *pero* | *(chien, mais)* |
| *turrón* **vs.** *turón* | *(nougat, putois)* |

**1.6** Ejercicio/Exercice

A few speakers trill French *r*; you can hear Édith Piaf trilling in the song *Non, je ne regrette rien* (widely available online). Most speakers, however, pronounce *r* as a fricative that is very similar to the Spanish pronunciation of the letters *g* (before *e*/*i*) and *j*. Notice where the letter *r* is and is not pronounced in the words below and then imitate what you hear.

*Il faut rester. (Hay que quedar.)*
*Roger, c'est rien. (Roger, no es nada.)*
*René, mon amour (René, mi amor)*
*repartir à zéro (partir desde cero)*
*C'est très rare. (Es muy raro.)*
*Nous sommes quatre frères. (Somos cuatro hermanos.)*

**Silent consonants in Spanish**
There are few silent letters in Spanish, and, once spelling rules have been learned, words can be pronounced right off the page. All consonants are pronounced, including consonants at the end of syllables and of words; the only silent consonant is *h*.

 **1.7** Ejercicio/Exercice

The *h* is not pronounced in these words in either language (though its presence between two vowels may mark a syllable boundary). Predict how these words will sound and then listen to them.

*alcohol ~ alcool*
*antihistamina ~ antihistaminique*
*deshidratar ~ déshydrater*
*hipótesis ~ hypothèse*
*hombre ~ homme*
*hoy ~ aujourd'hui*
*bah ~ bah*

**Silent consonants in French**
Many of the final consonants that are written in French are not pronounced. They once were, though, and orthography, which is very conservative, preserves earlier stages of the language. The paired names below show that when a final *e* ("unstable *e*," see 1C below) follows, the consonant is then pronounced.

| M | F |
|---|---|
| *Arnaud* | *Arnaude* |
| *Charlot* | *Charlotte* |
| *Christian* | *Christiane* |
| *Louis* | *Louise* |
| *Martin* | *Martine* |
| *Raymond* | *Raymonde* |
| *Simon* | *Simone* |

In the words above, the presence of the vowel *e* after the final consonant means that the consonant is pronounced. This is a way of understanding what happens in the phenomenon called LIAISON, when a word-final consonant, otherwise silent, is pronounced before a vowel in a following word. (Here again, a phenomenon that occurs within words in French also occurs within phrases.)

 *allez* vs. *Allez-y (Vámonos)*
*bon* vs. *un bon exemple (un buen ejemplo)*
*chez* vs. *chez elle (en casa de ella)*
*comment* vs. *Comment allez-vous? (¿Cómo les va?)*
*en* vs. *en hiver (en invierno)*
*est* vs. *Quelle heure est-il? (¿Qué hora es?)*
*les* vs. *les hommes (los hombres)*
*plus* vs. *plus en bas (más para abajo)*
*tout* vs. *tout à fait (en efecto)*
*trois* vs. *trois heures (tres horas)*

Liaison is becoming less frequent, and pronouncing all possible liaisons is a mark of formal, deliberate speech. According to current norms, it is required in conventional phrases (like *comment allez-vous* or *quelle heure est-il* above), or where the first word is unlikely to appear by itself (as with prepositions) or is closely allied to the next (as with articles before nouns). Liaison is optional in less tightly knit phrases; for example, the *s* in *pas encore* and *je suis en Amérique* may not be pronounced in casual speech. There are also cases where liaison cannot occur, even though a following word is pronounced with an initial vowel. In modern French *h* is not pronounced, but it once was and what is left of that pronunciation is the ability of some words beginning in *h* to block liaison. These words are conventionally marked in the dictionary with an asterisk, as in the list below. In grammar books, this liaison-blocking *h* is called *h aspiré*; the *h* that does not block liaison is called *h muet*.

 WITH LIAISON                          WITHOUT LIAISON
*l'hôtel (el hotel)*                        *la \*honte (la vergüenza)*
*les heures (las horas)*                    *les \*halles (los mercados)*

| | |
|---|---|
| des hommes *(unos hombres)* | des *héros *(unos héroes)* |
| nos habitudes *(nuestras costumbres)* | nos *hors-d'oeuvre *(nuestros entremeses)* |
| plus honnête *(más honesto)* | plus *haut *(más alto)* |
| très heureux *(muy feliz)* | très *hollandais *(muy holandés)* |

Many of the words that begin with *h aspiré* (i.e., that block liaison) are borrowed words, most of which begin with *ha-* or *ho-*, for example, *hamburger, hippie, hobby, hooligan* (from English); *halal, hammam, haschisch* (from Arabic).

## 1C. VOWELS

### Vowels in Spanish

Spanish has only five contrastive vowels: *a, e, i, o, u*. There are just as many vowels as there are letters in the alphabet to spell them, and each of these letters always represents the same sound. The pronunciation of vowels does vary slightly, depending on surrounding sounds, but these variations produce no change in meaning and are not reflected in spelling.

The vowels of Spanish are conventionally presented in a triangle that represents the movement of the tongue forward and back (left to right on the triangle) and up and down (top to bottom on the triangle). The slashes are used to indicate PHONEMES: classes of sounds that contrast with others in a given language. In addition to the movement of the tongue, the vowel sounds are distinguished from one another by

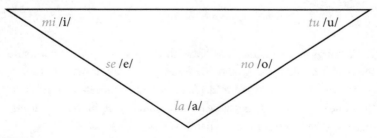

Figure 1.1

the position of the lips: stretched for the front vowels /e/ and /i/, and rounded for the back vowels /o/ and /u/. The vowel /a/ is pronounced with the tongue low and the mouth open.

Vowels in Spanish are pronounced regardless of their position in the word: at the beginning or the end, in stressed or unstressed syllables. When you read Spanish, you pronounce all of the vowels you see, with two exceptions. The letter *u* does not represent any sound when it comes between the letter *g* and *e* or *i*, as in *guerra* and *Guillermo* (French *guerre*, *Guillaume*). The *u* performs the same function in both languages: it is an orthographic indicator that the *g* is not pronounced like *j*. In Spanish words where *u* is pronounced between *g* and *e* or *i*, it is marked with the symbol ¨ to show this. An unpronounced *u* also comes between the letter *q* and *e* or *i*, as in *que* and *quien* (French *que*, *qui*); *u* is pronounced after *q* only in borrowed words like *quáker* and *quórum*.

 **1.8** Ejercicio/Exercice

Listen to these words and observe when the *u* is pronounced in Spanish and when it is not. Then repeat the words

*agüero* ~ *augure*
*águila* ~ *aigle*
*lingüista* ~ *linguiste*
*guardián* ~ *gardien*
*guía* ~ *guide*
*guitarra* ~ *guitare*
*quiosco* ~ *kiosque*

Diphthongs in Spanish are spelled with the two vowels that comprise them. (Recall that *guerra* and *Guillermo*, etc., contain no diphthongs because the *u* is not pronounced.) In some words, the letter *y* represents the same sound as *i* when it appears at the end of a diphthong or TRIPH-THONG (three vowels in one syllable).

**1.9** Ejercicio/Exercice

Listen to these words and observe that the written vowels of diphthongs and triphthongs are pronounced in Spanish. (The letter *y* is pronounced like *i* at the end of words.) Then repeat the words.

pat*io* (*patio*)
p*ue*rco (*porc*)
Uru*guay* (*Uruguay*)
c*au*sa (*cause*)
b*ai*le (*danse*)
*Eu*ropa (*Europe*)
h*ay* (*il y a*)
c*iu*dad (*ville*)
c*ui*dado (*soin*)

**Vowels in French**

The following section describes the simplest, and most colloquial, form of the French vowel system. It is possible to make even more distinctions than those described here, and some speakers of French equate more distinctions with higher prestige (just as some speakers of Spanish believe it is prestigious to distinguish the pronunciation of *c* and *z* from that of *s*). In any case, once you can make all the sounds described below, you can then learn to make any further distinctions.

In French, there are many more vowel sounds than there are letters in the alphabet to spell them. As a result, a vowel in French may be spelled by a combination of letters; what look like diphthongs or even triphthongs may be pronounced as simple vowels. When adjacent vowels do not belong to the same syllable, the symbol ¨ is used to show this:  mais (*pero*) vs. maïs (*maíz*).

The combinations of letters underlined below represent simple vowels in French, while in Spanish they are diphthongs:

 *air* (*aire*)
c*au*se (*causa*)

*euro (euro)*
*peigne (peine)*
*série (serie)*

The chart below is organized as for the Spanish vowels, with front-back movement of the tongue from left to right and up-down movement from top to bottom. Note the difference between slashes (used for phonemes) and brackets (used for sounds that belong to phoneme classes). The phonetic symbols are from the International Phonetic Alphabet (IPA). **There are four important differences between French vowels and Spanish vowels (in addition to the obvious fact that there are more of them). First, the French mid vowels (/e/, /ø/, and /o/) have two variants depending on what kind of syllable they are in.** In syllables that end in a pronounced vowel (open syllables), the vowel sound is higher and tenser ([e, ø, o]); in syllables that end in a pronounced consonant (closed syllables), the vowel is lower and laxer ([ɛ, œ, ɔ]). Listen to the words in the vowel chart to hear the contrast in the vowels of *thé* vs. *tête*, *peu* vs. *peur*, *peau* vs. *pomme*.

In Spanish, too, the mid vowels /e/ and /o/ vary slightly in pronunciation depending on whether they appear in an open or a closed syllable. In French, though, contrasts between one vowel and another have to be exaggerated because there are so many vowels, and each one has to

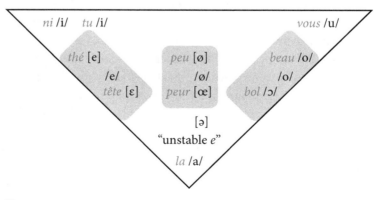

Figure 1.2

stake out its own territory in the "architecture" of the vowel system. And, the open and closed mid vowels are spelled differently from one another in French.

**The second difference is that in French there are front vowels pronounced with the lips rounded, [y], [ø], and [œ], in addition to front vowels pronounced with the lips stretched, [i], [e], and [ɛ].** Spanish has no front rounded vowels; speakers of Spanish automatically associate front vowels with stretched lips and may hear the vowel /y/, for example, as /i/.

🔊 ( **1.10** Ejercicio/Exercice )

Making the front rounded vowels takes some practice. To pronounce them, start with your tongue in the position of the unrounded vowel and then round your lips. Move your lips only, not your tongue!

[i] → → → [y]
[e] → → → [ø]

**The third difference is that there is a variant of *e* called unstable *e* that occurs in unstressed, open syllables.** Unstable *e* is a kind of vowel-in-waiting which is usually not pronounced but has the potential to be pronounced. Something similar happens in English, where the unstressed *e* of *int(e)resting* or *ev(e)ry* may be pronounced in careful speech. An unstable *e* at the end of a word signals that the consonant that precedes it is pronounced. Go back to the names listed on page 11 and observe that the *e* at the end of the feminine names signals that the consonant before it is pronounced.

In spelling, unstable *e* appears without accent marks and at the end of syllables. Here is how the three options for pronouncing the letter *e* in French are spelled:

[e]: *é* as in *vérité*; *e* as in *les*, *est*, *aller*, *allez* (in syllables spelled with a final unpronounced consonant); *ai* as in *arriverai*, *parlerai*

[ɛ]: *è* as in *mère*; *ê* as in *même*; *e* as in *personne*, *Mexique* (in syllables spelled with a final pronounced consonant; note that the *x* of *Mexique* is phonetically [ks])

[ə]: *e* as in *mere*, *même*, *personne*, *refaire*, *boulangerie* (in syllables spelled without a final consonant)

Unstable *e* is dropped whenever the consonants around it can be pronounced together—which is most of the time. In the words below, it would be pronounced only in extremely formal, meticulous speech.

*ach(e)ter*
*av(e)nue*
*boul(e)vard*
*charcut(e)rie*
*évén(e)ment*
*maint(e)nant*
*om(e)lette*

Detalles/Détails

Unstable *e* is sometimes pronounced in very emphatic speech, or in imitation of dialects in the south of France characterized by pronunciation of this vowel, or when an extra syllable is needed in song lyrics or poetry. In other words, unstable *e* is somehow "present" even when it is not pronounced. Of course, orthography—and the teaching of orthography—contribute to the presence of unstable *e* in the minds of speakers of French.

**1.11 Ejercicio/Exercice**

The loss of unstable *e* in French can make French words much shorter than their Spanish equivalents. Listen to the words below and observe that all of the vowels—stressed and unstressed—are pronounced in Spanish. Then practice pronouncing the words in both languages.

| | |
|---|---|
| *All(e)magne* (2 syllables) | *Alemania* (4 syllables) |
| *batt(e)rie* (2 syllables) | *batería* (4 syllables) |
| *brac(e)let* (2 syllables) | *brazalete* (4 syllables) |

*Cath(e)rine* (2 syllables)    *Caterina* (4 syllables)
*em(e)raude* (2 syllables)    *esmeralda* (4 syllables)
*lot(e)rie* (2 syllables)    *lotería* (4 syllables)
*méd(e)cine* (2 syllables)    *medicina* (4 syllables)

The loss of unstable *e* occurs in phrases as well as words. (It was pointed out above, in 1A, that stress in French often operates across phrases; here is another example of a phrase-level phenomenon.)

🔊 *C'est c(e) qu'on dit.*    *(Es lo que se dice.)*
*mon p(e)tit ami*    *(mi pequeño amigo)*
*On s(e) connaît.*    *(Uno se conoce.)*
*pas d(e) quoi*    *(de nada)*
*tout l(e) monde*    *(todo el mundo)*

**The fourth difference between French and Spanish vowels is nasality (produced by air resonating in the nasal cavity). In French—but not in Spanish—adding nasality to a vowel can change meaning.** Nasal vowels are audibly different from oral vowels, which are pronounced with air exiting through the mouth. The words below differ only in the oral/nasal contrast. (Variation in the pronunciation of a given nasal vowel—like that of all vowels—is due to surrounding sounds.)

🔊 /a/ vs. /ã/    *âge* vs. *ange* (*edad, ángel*)
*ça[†] va* vs. *savant* (*está bien, sabio*)
*la* vs. *l'an* (*la, el año*)
*papa* vs. *pampa* (*papá, pampa*)
/e/ vs. /ẽ/    *aigre* vs. *Ingres* (*agrio, Ingres*)
*fait* vs. *faim* (*hecho, hambre*)
*messe* vs. *mince* (*misa, delgado*)
*sept* vs. *sainte* (*siete, santa*)
/o/ vs. /õ/    *beau* vs. *bon* (*bello, bueno*)
*l'eau* vs. *long* (*el agua, largo*)
*dos* vs. *dont* (*espalda, del cual*)
*haute* vs. *honte* (*alta, vergüenza*)

[†] ç is pronounced like [s].

Look at how the words with nasal vowels are spelled. In each case, the nasal consonant, *n* or *m*, appears either at the end of a word or before another consonant. This spelling indicates that the nasal consonant itself is not pronounced but has "transferred" its nasality to the preceding vowel. (And notice, once more, that a single vowel sound in French can be spelled with two, or even three, letters.)

### Detalles/Détails

There is, in schoolbook French, one more nasal vowel: the nasalized counterpart of /ø/. It is not included here because its pronunciation is very close to that of /ē/ and most speakers pronounce it like that. The most common words containing this vowel are the masculine indefinite  article *un*, and the related *quelqu'un (alguien)*, *chacun (cada uno)*, and *aucun (ninguno)*, as well as words ending in -*un* and -*um*, like *commun (común)* and *parfum (perfume)*.

### 1.12 Ejercicio/Exercice

Listen to how the nasal vowels are pronounced in the names below (on the left) and notice that vowels are **not** nasal if the following nasal consonant is pronounced (on the right). Then imitate the pronunciation you hear.

| | |
|---|---|
| *Christian* | *Christiane* |
| *Jean* | *Jeanne* |
| *Fabien* | *Fabienne* |
| *Martin* | *Martine* |
| *Raymond* | *Raymonde* |
| *Simon* | *Simone* |

### Detalles/Détails

Except where there is liaison, most final consonants in French are not pronounced, except in borrowed words. Even final *m* and *n*, which usually nasalize preceding vowels and are not themselves pronounced (as in the exercise above), are pronounced in borrowed words: *rhum, maximum, barman, amen*.

Always pronounced: *-j, -k, -q* (words ending in these consonants are usually borrowed: *hadj, anorak, coq*)

Usually pronounced: *-b, -c, -f, -l, -r* (except in *-er* infinitives and *-er/-ier* suffixes: *aller, boulanger, chevalier*)

Usually silent: *-d, -g, -p, -s, -t, -x, -z* (most of the exceptions are borrowed words: *bled, grog, top, blues, basket, juke-box, fez*)

---

**Suggestions for further practice**

1. To become familiar with variations in pronunciation (including liaison in French), listen to a wide range of audio sources that include formal registers (e.g., newscasts, speeches, recited poetry) as well as dialogue and regional accents (e.g., interviews, scenes from films and TV shows).

2. The pronunciation of proper nouns—such as place names of indigenous origin in Latin America, family names drawn from regional languages in France, and *siglas/sigles* (nominalized acronyms)—is often unpredictable. Keep a list of people and places whose pronunciation you want to learn and ask a native speaker or use the pronunciation site www.forvo.com.

# *Chapter 2*

## ¿CÓMO SE CLASIFICAN Y SE DESCRIBEN LOS SUSTANTIVOS? COMMENT SE CLASSIFIENT ET SE DÉCRIVENT LES NOMS?

French and Spanish divide nouns, and the words that modify nouns, into two groups. In Latin, these groups were called "masculine" and "feminine," and this terminology (*masculino*/*masculin*, *femenino*/*féminin*) is still used. This grammatical distinction is called GENDER (*género*/*genre*), although, except for human beings and animals, nouns refer to entities that have no biological gender. The endings of nouns, and of their modifiers, often depend on which group they belong to.

### 2A. ARTICLES

Comparar/Comparer

*El hombre es un animal político.* (masculine) vs. *L'homme est un animal politique.* (neutral for gender)

When we say that a word "modifies" a noun, we mean that it adds nuances to the meaning of the noun. Definite and indefinite articles are modifiers that signify whether a noun is known (because it was mentioned previously or because it is common knowledge), or not. **In Spanish, the gender of a noun is clearly identified by the article: masculine nouns (m.) appear with masculine articles, feminine nouns (f.) with feminine articles.**

DEFINITE ARTICLES
IN SPANISH
singular: *el*† (m.), *la* (f.)
plural: *los* (m.), *las* (f.)

INDEFINITE ARTICLES
IN SPANISH
singular: *un* (m.), *una* (f.)
plural: *unos* (m.), *unas* (f.)

†The prepositions *a* and *de* combine with *el* to produce *al (a + el)* and *del (de + el)*.

**The articles in Spanish are always written as a separate word; they are never attached to the following noun, as can happen in French.** But, because consonants form syllables with following vowels in Spanish (and in French), the final consonant of the article may be heard as part of a following noun.

| | | |
|---|---|---|
| *el hada (la fée)* | sounds the same as | *helada (glacée)* |
| *las aves (les oiseaux)* | sounds the same as | *la sabes (tu la sais)* |

The nouns *hada* and *ave* above exemplify a minor exception to the generalization that the gender of nouns in Spanish is identified by the article. In Spanish, articles that end in *-a*, *la* and *una*, cannot appear next to singular nouns beginning with the stressed vowel [a]. *Hada* and *ave* are feminine nouns and are modified by feminine adjectives, but must appear after *el/un* in the singular: *el/un hada buena, el/un ave acuática*. This set of feminine nouns includes *agua, águila, área, habla,* and *hambre* (remember that *h* is not pronounced). The limitation does not apply to the plural articles (*las hadas buenas, unas aves acuáticas*) or to preceding adjectives (*la primera hada, una hermosa ave*).

**The interaction of the articles with nouns that begin with a vowel has a more general solution in French than in Spanish, where only** nouns beginning with stressed [a] are involved.

DEFINITE ARTICLES
IN FRENCH
singular: *le*† (m.), *la* (f.),
  *l'* (m. and f.)
plural: *les*† (m. and f.)

INDEFINITE ARTICLES
IN FRENCH
singular: *un* (m.), *une* (f.)

plural: *des* (m. and f.)

†The prepositions *à* and *de* combine with *le* to produce *au (à + le)* and *du (de + le)*, and with *les* to produce *aux (à + les)* and *des (de + les)*.

Both singular definite articles in French, *le* and *la*, end with a vowel, and both are shortened to *l'* before vowel-initial nouns. This phenomenon, called ELISION, makes it possible to use the definite article (but not the indefinite article) with vowel-initial nouns without knowing the noun's gender. Recall that *h* is not pronounced, so most words spelled with an initial *h* conform to this pattern because the first sound in the word is a vowel.

There are some nouns beginning with *h* that do not permit elision: *la haine*, *la harpe*, *le Havre*, *le héros*, etc. These nouns interact with the articles as if they began with a consonant, even though the *h* is not pronounced. This phenomenon, and the term *h aspiré*, are the legacy of a time when *h* was pronounced in French. It is standard practice in dictionaries to mark these nouns with an asterisk. (These same nouns block liaison with a preceding plural article, as explained in chapter 1B.)

**The plural articles do not show gender in French; they are the same for masculine and feminine.** In other words, you can use the plural definite or indefinite articles with a noun without knowing the noun's gender. The humorist David Sedaris learned to exploit this simplification when shopping in France: "I've started referring to everything in the plural, which can get expensive but has solved a lot of my problems" (from *Me Talk Pretty One Day*).

To sum up, there are three cases in French in which the articles do not reflect the gender of the noun they modify: (1) the singular definite article is *l'* before nouns beginning with a vowel or *h muet*, (2) the plural definite article is *les* for all nouns, and (3) the plural indefinite article is *des* for all nouns.

## 2B. GENDER

**The endings that reveal gender on nouns and adjectives are pronounced in Spanish; in French, many of these endings are not pronounced.**

Comparar/Comparer

 *el enemigo eterno/la enemiga eterna* (gender can be seen and heard) vs. *l'ennemi éternel/l'ennemie éternelle* (gender can be seen but not heard)

If you have mastered gender in Spanish or French, then you have a head start on learning it in the other language. For most COGNATES (words that share the same root), nouns that are feminine in one language are feminine in the other, and nouns that are masculine in one are masculine in the other. Only the few exceptions have to be learned. Some of the most common are listed below. (Remember that the indefinite article shows the gender of the noun in French, even when the reduced form of the definite article, *l'*, does not.)

| MASCULINE IN SPANISH | BUT | FEMININE IN FRENCH |
|---|---|---|
| *el análisis* | | *l'analyse/une analyse* |
| *el calor* | | *la chaleur* |
| *el equipo* | | *l'équipe/une équipe* |
| *el fin* | | *la fin* |
| *el mar* | | *la mer* |
| *el planeta* | | *la planète* |

| FEMININE IN SPANISH | BUT | MASCULINE IN FRENCH |
|---|---|---|
| *la cifra* | | *le chiffre* |
| *la leche* | | *le lait* |
| *la nariz* | | *le nez* |
| *la sangre* | | *le sang* |
| *la sal* | | *le sel* |
| *la sonrisa* | | *le sourire* |

You can find a more complete list of cognates with opposite genders online (just enter "French/Spanish gender differences" in a search engine).

Nouns with the same meaning do not have to be cognates, of course. *Bicicleta* and *vélo* are obviously not cognates, for example, nor are *helado* and *glace*. For noncognate words, you have to learn gender. The best approach is to associate nouns with their article (the indefinite article, in French) or with an adjective that shows gender (has audible gender, in French).

*una bicicleta italiana ~ un vélo italien*
*un helado delicioso ~ une glace délicieuse*

Another approach is to predict gender from the ending of nouns. This is easier in Spanish than in French, because the ending of words in Spanish has suffered less erosion over time. Here are some useful predictions.

FEMININE IN SPANISH
- nouns ending in *-a*, except *el día, el mapa, el clima,* and other words ending in *-ma*
- nouns ending in *-ción/-sión/-xión*: *nación, tensión, conexión*
- nouns ending in *-dad/-tad/-tud*: *ciudad, libertad, gratitud*
- nouns ending in *-sis/-itis*: *apendicitis, crisis, tesis,* but not *el análisis*
- nouns ending in *-z*: *paz, raíz, rapidez,* and other words ending in *-ez*, but not *el barniz, el lápiz*

MASCULINE IN SPANISH
- nouns ending in *-o*, except *la mano, la foto (fotografía), la moto (motocicleta)*
- nouns ending in *-l*: *ideal, local, pastel*
- nouns ending in *-n*: *avión, jabón, origen,* but not *la imagen, la razón*
- nouns ending in *-r*: *bar, error, sur*

There seems to be a contradiction between the generalizations that nouns ending in *-ción/-sion* are feminine and nouns ending in *-n* are (likely) masculine. However, *-ción* and *-sión* are suffixes, and suffixes trump letters in terms of gender classification. Suffixes—which, after all, are parts of words—are extremely reliable predictors of gender.

The gender of adjectives depends on the gender of the nouns they describe. In Spanish, singular adjectives ending in *-a* modify feminine nouns and adjectives ending in *-o* modify masculine nouns; adjectives ending in *-e* or a consonant can modify nouns of either gender.

**2.1 Ejercicio/Exercice**

Decide what form of the adjectives should modify the nouns in the following sentence. Note that some adjectives are invariable, but the article always indicates the gender of the noun.

*La semana* _____ *la Asamblea General llamó la atención del*
　　　　　*(pasado)*
*Consejo de Seguridad hacia una situación* _____
　　　　　　　　　　　　　　　　　*(político)*
_____ *de poner en peligro la seguridad* _____.
*(susceptible)*　　　　　　　　　　　　*(internacional)*

---

In French, a few final letters are reliable predictors of masculine gender:

- nouns ending in *-o*: *le lavabo, le verso, le zéro,* but *la météo (météorologie), la photo (photographie)*
- nouns ending in vowel + *-t*: *le chocolat, le ticket, le lit, le boulot, le but*
- nouns ending in *-c*: *le lac, le sac, le tabac*
- nouns ending in *-d*: *le fond, le froid, le pied*
- nouns ending in *-l*: *l'ail, le bol, le sommeil*

Gender is also predictable for a number of common suffixes. Where these French suffixes have Spanish equivalents, gender need not be learned (i.e., the masculine suffixes in French correspond to masculine suffixes in Spanish, and the feminine suffixes in French to feminine suffixes in Spanish).

FEMININE IN FRENCH
- nouns ending in *-ée*: *l'année, la journée, la nausée*
- nouns ending in *-tion/-sion (-ción/-sión)*: *la fiction, la nation, la tension*
- nouns ending in *-ade (-ada)*: *la limonade, la brigade, la croisade*
- nouns ending in *-ure (-ura)*: *l'architecture, la littérature, la nature*
- nouns ending in *-ine (-ina)*: *l'aspirine, la cantine, la médecine*
- nouns ending in *-ie (-ía)*: *l'épicerie, la géographie, la patrie*

MASCULINE IN FRENCH
- nouns ending in *-ment (-mento/-miento)*: *le fondement, le parlement, le supplément*
- nouns ending in *-ège/-age (-egio/-agio)*: *le collège, le privilège, le garage*

- nouns ending in *-isme (-ismo)*: *le capitalisme*, *le journalisme*, *le séisme*
- nouns ending in *-aire (-ero)*: *le dictionnaire*, *le commentaire*, **but** *la grammaire*

Many of the suffixes above, in both the feminine and masculine categories, end in *-e*. In other words, the letter *-e* is not a reliable marker of grammatical gender in French when used as part of a suffix. However, the MORPHEME *-e* is a marker of biological gender in French when added to nouns referring to males (*un Américain/une Américaine*), just as *-a* is in Spanish (*un americano/una americana*). When the final vowel is not a separate morpheme, however, it is not a predictor of gender. For example, the final vowels of *thérapeute* and *dentiste* in French, or *terapeuta* and *dentista* in Spanish, are part of longer morphemes and so do not denote gender. These nouns can refer to either males or females, and, grammatically, can be either masculine or feminine: *le/la thérapeute*, *le/la dentiste* (*cycliste, guitariste, perfectionniste, pessimiste, socialiste*); *el/la terapeuta*, *el/la dentista* (*ciclista, guitarrista, perfeccionista, pesimista, socialista*).

**Feminine adjectives in French must end in** *-e*. Masculine adjectives to which *-e* is added to form the feminine will undergo the phonetic changes described in chapter 1B. Here are some examples (note that the adjective *démocratique* has only one form, which ends in *-e*).

| | |
|---|---|
| *extérieur: la politique extérieure* | *(la política exterior)* |
| *français: la délégation française* | *(la delegación francesa)* |
| *étranger: la diplomatie étrangère* | *(la diplomacia extranjera)* |
| *actif: la population active* | *(la población activa)* |
| *démocratique: la république démocratique* | *(la república democrática)* |

## 2.2 Ejercicio/Exercice

Give the equivalent of the following noun phrases in French/Spanish:

la cooperación económica _____

_____ l'organisation internationale

el tratamiento desigual _____

_____ le mécanisme insutionnel

Detalles/Détails

Both French and Spanish have pairs of nouns with different meanings that differ only in gender and otherwise look the same. In some cases, both languages make the distinction with gender; in others, one language employs different words.

| FRENCH | SPANISH |
|---|---|
| *le livre (el libro)* vs. *la livre (la libra)* | *el capital (le capital)* vs. *la capital (la capitale)* |
| *le mode (el modo)* vs. *la mode (la moda)* | *el cava (le champagne)* vs. *la cava (la cave)* |
| *le poste (el puesto)* vs. *la poste (el correo)* | *el corte (la coupe)* vs. *la corte (la cour)* |
| *le tour (la vuelta)* vs. *la tour (la torre)* | *el mañana (le futur)* vs. *la mañana (le matin)* |
| *le voile (el velo)* vs. *la voile (la vela)* | *el Papa (le Pape)* vs. *la papa (la patate)* |

You may have come to the end of this section thinking, "How am I supposed to remember all this?" The answer is that awareness of the information above—not memorization of it—will help you notice the details of what you hear. Over time, you will master gender by hearing many, many nouns with their accompanying modifiers.

## 2C. NUMBER

**Pluralization of nouns and adjectives is similar in Spanish and French; the most important difference is that pluralization is usually inaudible in French.**

Comparar/Comparer

 *Los Miembros de las Naciones <u>Unidas</u> arreglarán sus controversias <u>internacionales</u> por medios <u>pacíficos</u>.* (number is audible on all the adjectives) vs. *Les Membres des Nations Unies règlent leurs différends <u>internationaux</u> par des moyens pacifiques.* (number is audible on only one adjective)

In Spanish, nouns and adjectives ending in a vowel are pluralized by adding -*s*. Spanish words cannot end in two consonants, so nouns and adjectives ending in a consonant are pluralized by adding -*es*. This additional syllable -*es* does not change where stress falls, because words ending in -*s* are stressed on the next-to-last syllable.

**2.3** Ejercicio/Exercice

Make the singular nouns and articles plural, and the plural nouns and articles singular. Notice that the plurals are stressed on the same syllable as the singulars.

| | | | | |
|---|---|---|---|---|
| *la ley* | → _____ | *las resoluciones* | → | _____ |
| *la agencia* | → _____ | *las agendas* | → | _____ |
| *el voto* | → _____ | *los países* | → | _____ |
| *el presidente* | → _____ | *los miembros* | → | _____ |

French, unlike Spanish, allows words to end in two consonants— at least in spelling. So, there is no need for two plural endings, and -*s* is added to most nouns and adjectives to form the plural. This pluralizing -*s* is not pronounced, except with liaison in certain circumstances (see chapter 1B). When the noun already ends in -*s*, no plural ending is added.

**2.4** Ejercicio/Exercice

Make the singular nouns and articles plural, and the plural nouns and articles singular. The written ending -*s* is inaudible in the plural of all of these nouns, though the plural form of the article makes pluralization—but not gender—clear. Note that nouns ending in -*s* in the singular, like *pays*, are invariable.

| | | | | |
|---|---|---|---|---|
| *la loi* | → _____ | *les résolutions* | → | _____ |
| *l'agence* | → _____ | *les agendas* | → | _____ |

| | | | | |
|---|---|---|---|---|
| *le vote* | → _____ | *les pays* | → | _____ |
| *le président* | → _____ | *les membres* | → | _____ |

The simplicity of the French rule for pluralization is complicated by the existence of several minor patterns for plurals. The example below illustrates several of the most common.

*Les journaux* (sg. *journal*) *ont publié les travaux* (sg. *travail*) *de la commission et les principaux* (sg. *principal*) *discours* (sg. *discours*) *de ses membres.*

*(Los periódicos han publicado los trabajos de la comisión y los principales discursos de sus miembros.)*

Of course, there are exceptions to these exceptions. Not all adjectives ending in *-al* are irregular; *fatal*, for example, is perfectly regular (pl. *fatals*). Consult a reference grammar to see all of the possibilities.

## 2D. DEMONSTRATIVE AND POSSESSIVE ADJECTIVES

| Demonstrative adjectives in Spanish | | Demonstrative adjectives in French | |
|---|---|---|---|
| (m. sg.) | (f. sg.) | (m. sg.) | (f. sg.) |
| *este, ese, aquel* | *esta, esa, aquella* | *ce/cet*[†] | *cette* |
| (m. pl.) | (f. pl.) | (m. and f. pl.) | |
| *estos, esos, aquellos* | *estas, esas, aquellas* | *ces* | |

The first form listed for Spanish is used to indicate proximity to the speaker; the following forms indicate increasing distance. In French, the words *ci* and *là* (cognate with *aquí* and *allá*) are added to show proximity and distance, respectively, for example, *cette femme-ci* (close) vs. *cette femme-là* (far).

[†]We have already seen this pattern: nouns that begin with a vowel sound in French must be preceded by modifiers that end in an audible consonant (e.g., m. *ce moment*, *cet instant*).

| Possessive adjectives in Spanish | Possessive adjectives in French |
|---|---|
| **for singular possessors:** | **for singular possessors:** |
| (sg.) | (m. sg.) |
| *mi, tu, su* | *mon, ton, son* |
| | (f. sg.) |
| | *ma/mon[†], ta/ton, sa/son* |
| (pl.) | (m. and f. pl.) |
| *mis, tus, sus* | *mes, tes, ses* |
| **for plural possessors:** | **for plural possessors:** |
| (sg.) | (m. and f. sg.) |
| *nuestro/-a, (vuestro, -a[††]), su* | *notre, votre, leur* |
| (pl.) | (m. and f. pl.) |
| *nuestros, -as, (vuestros, -as[††]), sus* | *nos, vos, leurs* |

Forms are listed in first person, second person, third person order.

[†]Once again, the forms ending in a consonant appear before nouns that begin with a vowel sound. As a result, in pairs such as *mon ami/mon amie (mi amigo/mi amiga)* the contrast between masculine and feminine can be made in writing but cannot be heard.
[††]The forms of Spanish *vuestro* are in parentheses because they are used only in Spain, not in Latin America. For a discussion of this phenomenon, see chapter 3H.


Except for Spanish *nuestro* (and *vuestro*), the possessive adjectives in the chart above cannot be used for emphasis or contrast (the way the possessive can be stressed in English *That's my car*). In Spanish, the forms that can be stressed are PRONOUNS and have two syllables. (Other pronouns are discussed in chapter 3.) Note that *suyo* corresponds to singular *él, ella*, and *usted* as well as to plural *ellos, ellas*, and *ustedes*.

*Es mío/mía, tuyo/tuya, suyo/suya, (vuestro/-a), nuestro/-a*
*Son míos/mías, tuyos/tuyas, suyos/suyas, (vuestros/-as), nuestros/-as*

In French, there are two possibilities for emphatic/contrastive possessives. One option is to use the stressable forms of the subject pronouns, *moi, toi, lui, elle, nous, vous, eux, elles* (see chapter 3A), after the preposition *à*:

*C'est/ce sont à moi, toi, lui, elle, nous, vous, eux, elles*

The other option is to use the possessive pronouns:

*C'est le mien/la mienne, le tien/la tienne, le sien/la sienne, le/la vôtre,*
   *le/la nôtre, le/la leur*
*Ce sont les miens/les miennes, les tiens/les tiennes, les siens/les siennes,*
   *les vôtres, les nôtres, les leurs*

**2.5  Ejercicio/Exercice**

Complete each of the sentences below with the demonstrative or possessive adjective that corresponds to the underlined word in the other language.

*<u>Cet</u> accord entre _____ pays est essentiel.*
*_____ acuerdo entre <u>nuestros</u> países es esencial.*
*Les ambassadeurs ont apposé <u>leur</u> signature sur _____*
   *documents.*
*Los embajadores han puesto _____ firma en <u>estos</u>*
   *documentos.*
*Elle a posé _____ question à <u>ce</u> candidat-<u>ci.</u>*
*Ella le hizo <u>su</u> pregunta a _____ candidato.*
*_____ politique extérieure n'admet pas <u>cette</u> possibilité-<u>là.</u>*
*<u>Nuestra</u> política exterior no admite _____ posibilidad.*

**Suggestions for further practice**
   1. Choose a news article in French or Spanish and highlight all of the nouns. Then identify the ones with suffixes that indicate gender and/or the ones whose gender can be determined through context (adjective agreement, articles, pronouns, etc.).
   2. Compare the use of direct and indirect articles on the French and Spanish home pages of a multilingual website (e.g., the United Nations: www.un.org/fr/index.html and www.un.org/es /index.html).

# Chapter 3

## ¿CÓMO FUNCIONAN LOS PRONOMBRES? COMMENT S'EMPLOIENT LES PRONOMS?

*Pronoun* is traditionally defined as a word that takes the place of a noun. In Spanish and French, there are different pronouns depending on the function of the noun in the sentence: subject, direct object, indirect object, reflexive object.

### 3A. SUBJECTS AND SUBJECT PRONOUNS

Comparar/Comparer
*Muchos padres ayudan a sus hijos a hacer sus tareas para que [ ] saquen buenas notas.* **vs.** *Beaucoup de parents aident leurs enfants à faire leurs devoirs pour qu'ils obtiennent de bonnes notes.*

**There are more subject pronouns in the second person in Spanish than in French**—though not all of them are used in any one dialect (see section 3H). The second-person pronouns *usted* and *ustedes*, which can be written *Ud.* and *Uds.*, developed from the use of the third person to express respect and so are used with third-person verbs.

Detalles/Détails
In many cultures, distance is equated with formality and respect, and proximity with informality and intimacy. In language, one way of showing respect is to address hearers in the third person, as if they were distant from the speaker. The pronoun *usted* in Spanish has its origin in the honorific *Vuestra Merced*, which—like *Votre Excellence* in

Table 3.1

| | Spanish subject pronouns | | French subject pronouns | |
|---|---|---|---|---|
| | (The formal/informal distinction in the second person is labeled for/inf.) | | | |
| | 1 sg. *yo* | 1 pl. *nosotros/nosotras* | 1 sg. *je/moi†* | 1 pl. *nous†* |
| Latin America | 2 sg. inf. *tú/vos* | 2 pl *ustedes* | | |
| | 2 sg. for. *usted* | | 2 sg. inf. *tu/toi†* | |
| Spain | 2 sg. inf. *tú* | 2 pl. inf. *vosotros/vosotras* | | 2 pl. *vous* |
| | 2 sg. for. *usted* | 2 pl. for. *ustedes* | 2 sg. for. *vous* | |
| | 3 sg. *él/ella* | 3 pl. *ellos/ellas* | 3 sg. *il/lui, elle†* | 3 pl. *ils/eux, elles†* |

†*Je, tu, il*, and *ils* are replaced by *moi, toi, lui,* and *eux,* respectively, when stressed; *nous, vous, elle,* and *elles* can be stressed.

French—addresses the hearer in the third person and requires the use of third-person verbs.

Spanish and French differ in how subject pronouns are used. In both languages, verb endings reflect subjects; in other words, the subject "governs" the person/number of the verb. In theory, verb endings should suffice to identify the subject—and in Spanish they do. Subject pronouns are used in Spanish to avoid confusion (especially in the third person, where third-person verb forms are used with second-person *usted* and *ustedes*) or to highlight the subject. For example, the subject pronoun must be used when it is the answer to a question.

*¿Quién escribió esto?*
*Lo escribí yo.*

In French, in contrast, conjugated verbs must have an overt subject. As discussed in chapter 4A, many verb forms sound the same, even though they differ in spelling, and the subject pronouns make it possible to distinguish one from another. To emphasize the subject, then, French must use an additional pronoun, since the subject pronoun is already present.

*Qui a écrit ça?*
*Moi, je l'ai écrit./C'est moi qui l'ai écrit.*

Some of the subject pronouns in French—*je*, *tu*, *il*, and *ils*—are CLIT-ICS: they can appear with the verb but cannot be used alone or carry stress. When a question requires a one-word answer, for example, DIS-JUNCTIVE pronouns must be used. So, the question *Qui va répondre?* can be answered *moi*, *toi*, *lui*, *elle*, *nous*, *vous*, *eux*, or *elles*. In Spanish, any of the subject pronouns can be one-word answers to the question *¿Quién va a contestar?* In other words, the Spanish subject pronouns are not clitics.

( **3.1** Ejercicio/Exercice )

Read the following study tips from a French-speaking student and then decide whether subject pronouns are necessary in the Spanish version.

*Si je ne comprends pas le concept que le professeur est en train d'ex-pliquer, je lui demande de le répéter. Quand je prends des notes, je souligne les points importants et puis je formule des questions basées sur ces points.*

*Si* _____ *no entiendo el concepto que está explicando el profe-sor,* _____ *le pido repetirlo. Cuando* _____ *tomo apuntes,* _____ *subrayo los puntos importantes y luego* _____ *formulo preguntas basadas en esos puntos.*

In the first and second persons, pronouns do not replace nouns but, rather, refer directly to the speaker and hearer. In the third person, subject pronouns actually replace nouns. If the noun refers to a human/ animate being, a pronoun can replace it in both languages.

*Mi profesora llegó tarde.* → *Ella llegó tarde.*
*Ma professeur est arrivée en retard.* → *Elle est arrivée en retard.*

When the subject of the verb is a thing (i.e., not animate), the two languages behave differently. A noun referring to a thing cannot be replaced with a subject pronoun in Spanish. To avoid repetition, the noun is simply left out.

*La lección es demasiado larga.* → *Es demasiado larga.*

Since it's not possible to have a subjectless verb in French, a subject pronoun must be present whether the referent of the pronoun is animate or not.

*La leçon est trop longue.* → *Elle est trop longue./C'est trop long.*

In French, the pronoun *ce* and *ça* are very common replacements for inanimate subjects. (*Ce* and *ça* are discussed in section 3G.)

The requirement that a conjugated verb have an overt subject is so strong in French that there must be a subject pronoun even when there's nothing for it to refer to.

*Il fait froid dans la salle de classe.*

English has the same requirement; the pronoun *it* in the sentence *It's cold in the classroom* doesn't replace anything, but it must be present. *\*Fait froid* and *\*Is cold* are not possible sentences (as indicated by the asterisks). The Spanish equivalent, *Hace frío,* simply has no subject (third-person singular is the unmarked form of the verb).

### Detalles/Détails

Both English and French have a rule that conjugated verbs must have an overt subject, and similar exceptions to that rule. In conjoined sentences, the subject is required only with the first verb.

*I usually come home, [ ] have a snack, and [ ] do my homework.* ~
  *D'habitude, je rentre chez moi, [ ] prends un goûter et [ ] fais mes devoirs.*

### *On* in French

In addition to its use as an impersonal pronoun (see chapter 3E), *on* is used in spoken French as a substitute for both the first and second persons. Depending on context, the sentence below could be understood to refer to the speaker(s) or to address the hearer(s).

*On est très confortable ici.* ~ *Estoy/estamos/estás/está/están muy cómodo(s) aquí.*

The use of *on* as a substitute for *nous* is so routine in spoken French that it is common to hear sentences like *On cherche nos places (Buscamos nuestros asientos)*, in which the possessive *nos* refers to a *nous* that is not there.

### 3B. DIRECT OBJECTS AND DIRECT-OBJECT PRONOUNS

### Comparar/Comparer

*Los estudiantes vieron al profesor en la calle.* **vs.** *Les étudiants ont vu [ ] le professeur dans la rue.*

When the subject of a sentence performs an action directly on some entity, that entity is called the direct object (DO). Entities that are acted upon are usually things: walls are painted, food is cooked, etc. Direct objects can be people, but people are more likely to perform actions than to be acted upon. For this reason, only a minority of direct objects are human, and in Spanish they are marked: when the direct object

Table 3.2

| Spanish direct-object pronouns | | French direct-object pronouns | |
|---|---|---|---|
| 1 sg. *me* | 1 pl. *nos* | 1 sg. *me/moi*[†] | 1 pl. *nous* |
| 2 sg. *te* | 2 pl. (*os*) | 2 sg. *te/toi*[†] | 2 pl. *vous* |
| 3 sg. *lo/la* | 3 pl. *los/las* | 3 sg. *le/la* | 3 pl. *les* |

[†] in affirmative commands

is a noun that refers to a specific human being, it is marked with the preposition *a* (often called *a personal*). There is no equivalent of this in French, as you can see in the French sentence above.

The direct-object pronouns in the two languages look very similar except for the gender distinction in the third-person plural in Spanish. In French, there is only one direct-object pronoun in the third-person plural, just as there is only one definite article in the plural: *les*.

In addition to referring to singular, masculine direct objects, Spanish *lo* and French *le* have another function: they can be used to refer to situations, events, or ideas that correspond to no specific noun, and so have no gender. Used in this way, they are called NEUTER pronouns.

*El profesor se siente orgulloso de sus estudiantes, pero no lo dice.* ~
*Le professeur se sent fier de ses étudiants, mais il ne le dit pas.*

In Spanish, there is a corresponding neuter subject pronoun, *ello*; in French, *ça* serves this function.

**3.2** Ejercicio/Exercice

Each French sentence below contains an underlined direct-object pronoun. Decide which pronoun to use in the corresponding Spanish sentences. As you do this, notice that in French the participles agree with preceding direct objects in gender and number.

*Je cherche mon agrafeuse.*      *Busco mi grapadora.*
    *L'as-tu vue?*                 ¿_____ has visto?

| | |
|---|---|
| *Je cherche mes crayons.* | *Busco mis lápices.* |
| <u>Les</u> as-tu <u>vus</u>? | ¿_____ has visto? |
| *Je cherche mon portable.* | *Busco mi móvil.* |
| <u>L'</u>as-tu <u>vu</u>? | ¿_____ has visto? |
| *Je cherche mes clés.* | *Busco mis llaves.* |
| <u>Les</u> as-tu <u>vues</u>? | ¿_____ has visto? |

## 3C. INDIRECT OBJECTS AND INDIRECT-OBJECT PRONOUNS

There are situations in which the action of the verb goes beyond the direct object. Situations such as giving/taking, lending/borrowing, sending, and teaching involve not only what is given/taken, etc., but also a third party: the indirect object (IO). The indirect object is usually a person (unlike the direct object, which is usually a thing) who is affected by a situation. The indirect nature of the effect is signaled by the preposition *a/à* that precedes the indirect object when it appears as a noun or a stressed pronoun. In Spanish, indirect objects often appear twice: once as clitics (*me*, etc.) and again as nouns or stressed pronouns (*mí*, etc.) after the preposition *a*. In the sentence below, *le* = *a mi hermano*. This doubling of the indirect object is not common in French.

*Le di el libro a mi hermano.* ~ *J'ai donné le livre à mon frère.*

Doubling of the indirect object is not required, and *Le di el libro* is perfectly grammatical. It is not possible, however, to say \**Di el libro a mi hermano*, as in French.

Table 3.3

| Spanish IO pronouns | | French IO pronouns | |
|---|---|---|---|
| 1 sg. *me* (*a mí*) | 1 pl. *nos* (*a nosotros*) | 1 sg. *me* (*moi*[†]) | 1 pl. *nous* |
| 2 sg. *te* (*a ti*) | 2 pl. (*os*) (*a vosotros*) | 2 sg. *te* (*toi*[†]) | 2 pl. *vous* |
| 3 sg. *le* (*a él/ella/Ud.*) | 3 pl. *les* (*a ellos/ellas/ Uds.*) | 3 sg. *lui* | 3 pl. *leur* |

[†] in affirmative commands

In both languages, indirect-object pronouns are used to express a wide range of indirect ways in which a person can be involved in a situation. For example, a mother might say to a child *Acábame tu plato/Finis-moi ton assiette*, where the benefit to the speaker is encoded as *me/moi* (*for me* in English).

**3.3** Ejercicio/Exercice

Match the Spanish sentences in the student dialogue below with their French equivalents and observe the differences in the underlined indirect-object pronouns. Note that the indirect object appears twice in the Spanish sentence *Porque al autor le dieron el Nobel*, but that this doubling does not occur in French.

A: *¡A mí me parece absurda esta novela!*

*Parce qu'on a donné le Nobel à l'auteur.*

B: *A mí también. Me da dolor de cabeza.*

*Tu es vraiment cynique, toi!*

A: *¿Por qué nos la recomendó la profe, entonces?*

*Ce roman me paraît absurde!*

B: *Porque al autor le dieron el Nobel.*

*Alors, pourquoi est-ce que la prof nous l'a recommandé?*

A: *¡Qué cínico eres!*

*A moi aussi, ça me donne mal à la tête.*

Detalles/Détails

In Spanish, the *a* that marks human direct objects makes them look like indirect objects. So, in some dialects the indirect-object pronouns *le* and *les* are used to refer to human direct objects. There are several variations on this possibility; a common one substitutes *le* for masculine direct objects.

*Vi al profesor.* → *Le vi.*

## 3D. REFLEXIVE PRONOUNS

In the charts in the previous sections, you can see that the direct- and indirect-object pronouns are the same for first person and second person in Spanish and in French: *me, te, nos, (os)*; *me, te, nous, vous*. The direct/indirect-object distinction is made only in the third person. Reflexive pronouns, used when the subject of a sentence is the same as either the direct or the indirect object, continue this trend: the direct/indirect/reflexive distinction is made only in the third person. In both languages, the third-person reflexive pronoun is *se/se*, and the corresponding stressable pronoun is *sí/soi*.

*Los estudiantes se acuestan muy tarde.* ~ *Les étudiants se couchent très tard.*

*Se/se* does not change for masculine/feminine or for singular/plural. The fact that this pronoun has neither gender nor number makes it ideal for use as an impersonal subject, a role that it plays in both languages (see chapter 4E).

## 3E. PRONOUN ORDER

Comparar/Comparer

*¿Se puede ser surrealista sin saber<u>lo</u>?* vs. *On peut être surréaliste sans <u>le</u> savoir?* (from Parallel Texts)

In Spanish, unstressed pronouns appear in the order indirect-direct before conjugated verbs. In the case of compound verbs that end in an infinitive or gerund, it is also possible to place them (in the same order) at the end of the compound. The accent marks show that stress remains on the same syllable after the pronouns are attached.

*Te* (IO) *lo* (DO) *muestro.*
*Te lo voy a mostrar./Voy a mostrártelo.*
*Te lo estoy mostrando./Estoy mostrándotelo.*

Combining the third-person-indirect-object pronouns *le* and *les* with any direct-object pronoun produces the transformation of *le/les* to *se*.

*Se lo muestro (a él/ella/usted/ellos/ustedes).*

Because of the substitution of *se* for *le/les* (which is the result of a long-ago change in pronunciation), the pronoun *se* has three functions in Spanish: (1) as a variant of *le/les*, (2) as a third-person reflexive pronoun, and (3) as an impersonal subject pronoun.

If you're learning French, you need to learn the order of the pronouns and where pronouns are placed in various kinds of sentences. In all but affirmative commands (see chapter 5C), object pronouns are ordered as follows: *me*, *te*, *nous*, *vous*, and *se* appear first; then *le*, *la*, and *les*; then *lui* and *leur*; followed by *y* and then *en* (these two pronouns are discussed in chapter 6B). This order is not based on whether the pronoun is a direct or an indirect object, as in Spanish.

*Je te* (IO) *le* (DO) *montre.*
*Je vais te le montrer.*
*Je suis en train de te le montrer.*

Notice two things: (1) the pronouns appear before the infinitive in French, where they cannot appear in Spanish, and (2) French does not have a progressive form equivalent to *estar* + gerund in Spanish to talk about what is happening at the moment of speech.

In the examples above, the order of the pronouns is the same in both languages. But, if third-person *lui* is substituted for *te*, the languages diverge. *Le* precedes *lui* according to French pronoun order, and *se* precedes *lo* in Spanish IO-DO order.

*Je le lui montre.* ~ *Se lo muestro.* (*le* has become *se*)

## 3.4 Ejercicio/Exercice

Match each Spanish sentence in this professor/student dialogue with its French equivalent. As you do this, observe that in French the direct-object pronouns are reduced and attached to the following verb when the verb begins with a vowel.

| | | |
|---|---|---|
| P: | *¿Ya lo hiciste?* | *Tu dois le faire comme ça.* |
| E: | *No, porque no lo entiendo.* | *Je vais te l'expliquer.* |
| P: | *Te lo voy a explicar/Voy a explicártelo.* | *Tu l'as fait?* |
| E: | *Lo puedo entender/Puedo entenderlo hasta aquí.* | *Ah! Maintenant laissez-moi le finir tout seul.* |
| P: | *Tienes que hacerlo así.* | *Je peux le comprendre jusque-là.* |
| E: | *¡Ah! Ahora déjeme terminarlo solo.* | *Non, parce que je ne le comprends pas.* |

## 3F. RELATIVE PRONOUNS

### Comparar/Comparer

*El muchacho que levantó la mano es muy inteligente.* **vs.** *Le garçon qui a levé la main est très intelligent.*

When a repeated noun is removed from a modifying clause, it is replaced by a relative pronoun. In Spanish, the "universal relativizer" is *que*, which is used to refer to either people or things, and as a substitute for either subjects or objects.

*Es el escritor/el libro que ganó el premio.* (**subject of** *ganó*)
*El escritor/el libro que eligieron es turco.* (**direct object of** *eligieron*)

French has two monosyllabic relative pronouns, *que* and *qui*. *Qui* is used when its antecedent is the subject of the relative clause—whether animate or inanimate.

*C'est l'écrivain/le livre qui a gagné le prix.* (**subject of** *a gagné*)

*Que* is used when the noun removed from the relative clause is the direct object of the clause—whether animate or inanimate. (Notice that *que* is reduced to *qu'* before a word that begins with a vowel sound.)

*L'écrivain/le livre <u>qu'</u>ils ont choisi est turc.* (**direct object of** *ont choisi*)

---

**3.5** Ejercicio/Exercice

Decide which relative pronoun, *que/qu'* or *qui*, to use in French.

| | |
|---|---|
| *La sección <u>que</u> quieres está llena.* | *La section _____ tu veux est pleine.* |
| *Los estudiantes <u>que</u> han terminado pueden irse.* | *Les étudiants _____ ont fini peuvent partir.* |
| *Es la película <u>que</u> vimos en clase.* | *C'est le film _____ on a vu en classe.* |
| *Tengo una pregunta <u>que</u> es bastante breve.* | *J'ai une question _____ est assez courte.* |
| *Ella es la estudiante <u>que</u> acaba de entrar.* | *C'est l'étudiante _____ vient d'entrer.* |

---

In order to be comprehensible, complex sentences must contain clues that can be used to decipher their meaning. In the case of relative clauses, Spanish and French use different, but equally comprehensible, clues. In the Spanish examples below, *hermana (soeur)* is the subject of some clauses and the direct object of others. The personal *a* preceding *hermana* identifies this noun as a direct object in the first sentence. In the second sentence, the lack of *a* before *hermana* identifies it as the subject of *conoce* even though it follows the verb. Verb-subject order is normal in subordinate clauses in Spanish.

*Es el escritor que conoce a mi hermana.* **vs.** *Es el escritor que conoce mi hermana.*

There is no personal *a* in French, and subjects and objects are distinguished by contrasting relative pronouns. Subjects (*écrivain* in the first sentence) are replaced by *qui*; direct objects (*écrivain* in the second sentence) are replaced by *que*.

> *C'est l'écrivain qui connait ma soeur.* **vs.** *C'est l'écrivain que ma soeur connait.*

In both languages, the simpler the role of the relative pronoun in the relative clause, the simpler the relative pronoun. In other words, additional information on relative pronouns, such as gender and number, is used to clarify the function of the relative pronoun. The relative pronouns *quien/quienes* are used in Spanish to refer to people, but only when preceded by prepositions.

> *Los compañeros con quienes estudiamos tendrán éxito.*

In French, invariable *qui* is used to refer to people after prepositions.

> *Les camarades avec qui nous étudions auront du succès.*

French has a relative pronoun, *dont*, that does not exist in Spanish. *Dont* replaces the prepositional phrase *de* + relative pronoun *que* (as *en*, discussed in chapter 6B, replaces *de* + noun).

> *J'ai lu le livre <u>dont</u> tu m'as parlé.* ~ *He leído el libro <u>de que</u> me hablaste.*

The preposition *de* is used in French to express possession, so *dont* also has this use. The equivalent of possessive *dont* is the adjective *cuyo* in Spanish (though *cuyo* is little used in informal, spoken language).

> *L'écrivain <u>dont</u> le livre a été choisi est turc.* ~ *El escritor <u>cuyo</u> libro fue elegido es turco.*

Detalles/Détails

In formal written texts, relative-clause sentences can be very complex. Relative pronouns like *las cuales* and *lesquelles* in the sentences below have gender and number, which helps to identify the noun that they refer to.

*Uno de los principales objetivos de la educación debe ser ampliar las ventanas <u>por las cuales</u> vemos al mundo.* vs. *Un des objectifs principaux de l'éducation doit être d'élargir les fenêtres à travers <u>lesquelles</u> nous voyons le monde.*

## 3G. DEMONSTRATIVE PRONOUNS

Demonstrative pronouns—like *this* or *that* in English—are used to refer to things (and, sometimes pejoratively, people) according to their proximity or distance from the speaker. The Spanish demonstratives fall into three sets, though the most distant is less used than the other two. The singular pronouns ending in -*o*, *esto*, *eso aquello*, are neuter pronouns, which means that they have no gender. (The direct-object pronoun *lo* can be both masculine and neuter, but, in the demonstrative set, masculine and neuter are separate.) The members of the distant sets can also be used pejoratively in both Spanish and French.

SPANISH DEMONSTRATIVE PRONOUNS

| CLOSE | FAR | FARTHER |
|---|---|---|
| sg. *este/esta/esto* | sg. *ese/esa/eso* | sg. *aquel/aquella/aquello* |
| pl. *estos/estas* | pl. *esos/esas* | pl. *aquellos/aquellas* |

There are only two sets in French.

FRENCH DEMONSTRATIVE PRONOUNS

| CLOSE | FAR |
|---|---|
| sg. *celui-ci/celle-ci (ceci/ça)* | sg. *celui-là/celle-là (cela/ça)* |
| pl. *ceux-ci/celles-ci* | pl. *ceux-là/celles-là* |

Notice that the pronoun *ça* is the short form of both *ceci* and *cela*, which are themselves the short forms of the compound demonstratives. *Ça* is used in many expressions in the spoken language as a neuter pronoun, as in the ubiquitous *Ça va?* (*¿Todo bien?*)

**3.6** Ejercicio/Exercice

Match each of the *ça* expressions with its Spanish equivalent. Notice that the expressions in Spanish have no subject pronoun.

| | |
|---|---|
| *Ça ne fait rien.* | *Me es igual.* |
| *Ça suffit.* | *Hace tiempo.* |
| *Ça fait longtemps.* | *Basta.* |
| *Ça vaut la peine.* | *Se ve.* |
| *Ça m'est égal.* | *Depende.* |
| *Ça se voit.* | *No pasa nada.* |
| *Ça dépend.* | *Vale la pena.* |

One might expect *ce* to be the short form of *ceci*, and *ce* does exist in French, of course. It is a demonstrative adjective (see chapter 2D) and a placeholder subject of *être*.

*C'est ça que je voulais dire.* ~ *Es eso lo que quería decir.*

A crucial difference between *ce* and *ça*, as shown in the example above, is that only the latter can be stressed. *Ça*, then, can be used to emphasize the unstressed subject *ce* (just as *moi* can be used to emphasize unstressed *je*, etc.).

**3.7** Ejercicio/Exercice

*Ce* (reduced to *c'* before words beginning with a vowel) appears before the verb *être* to comply with the rule that conjugated verbs must have a subject in French. Match the French expressions on the left with their equivalents in Spanish.

| | |
|---|---|
| *C'est qui?* | *Soy yo.* |
| *C'est moi.* | *Es lo mismo.* |
| *C'était nécessaire.* | *Es verdad.* |
| *C'est la même chose.* | *Es mejor.* |
| *C'est mieux.* | *Es una lástima.* |
| *C'est vrai.* | *Era necesario.* |
| *C'est dommage.* | *¿Quién es?* |

### Detalles/Détails

In French, it is normal to say *C'est moi/toi/lui/elle/nous/vous/eux/elles*, just as in English we say English *It's me/you/him/her/us/them*. And, similar to the prescriptive *It is I/he/she* (but not \**It's we/they*), French has *Ce sont eux/elles* (but not \**Ce sommes nous/C'êtes vous*).

### 3H. FORMS OF ADDRESS

In order to speak to someone in Spanish or French, you have to decide whether your relationship is formal/distant or informal/close. The relevant pronouns follow from this decision.

The number of second-person pronouns (and corresponding verb forms) is greater in Spanish than in French. However, not all of the possible second-person subject pronouns are used in any given dialect of Spanish—which means, in practical terms, that you should learn the system of a specific dialect. European Spanish has the greatest number of options, with a formal/informal distinction in both the singular and the plural. In Spain today, however, *vosotros* is gaining ground at the expense of *ustedes*, which is used in a shrinking number of situations.

singular: *tú* (informal) vs. *usted* (formal)
plural: *vosotros/vosotras* (informal) vs. *ustedes* (formal)

If *El pastor mentiroso* were told in European Spanish, the shepherd would address the villagers as *vosotros*, and use the indirect-object pronoun *os* and the command form *venid*.

*"¡El lobo!" gritó el pastorcito. "¡Os lo juro, es el lobo! ¡Venid corriendo!"*

In American Spanish (i.e., for the great majority of Spanish speakers), all plural hearers are addressed as *ustedes*. This does not mean that American speakers treat everyone formally; it means that there is no distinction in the plural.

*"¡El lobo!" gritó el pastorcito. "¡Se lo juro, es el lobo! ¡Vengan rápido!"*

The singular second-person pronoun used in Latin America varies by dialect; in Mexico and the Caribbean it is *tú*.

singular: *tú* (informal) vs. *usted* (formal)
plural: *ustedes*

In much of Central America and (especially southern) South America, the singular second-person pronoun is *vos* (not to be confused with the plural *vosotros*, used only in Spain).

singular: *vos* (informal) vs. *usted* (formal)
plural: *ustedes*

Adoption of *tú/vos* is an ongoing process in Latin America; as a result, there are countries in which both *tú* and *vos* are heard. With the exception of the subject pronouns, the pronouns that correspond to *vos* are the same as for *tú*, but in the verb system there are distinct *vos* forms for the present indicative and subjunctive and the commands (see the verb charts at the end of the book).

The French system, in contrast, has only two forms.

singular: *tu* (formal) vs. *vous* (formal)
plural: *vous*

Deciding which form of address to use is a sensitive matter. In much of the Spanish-speaking world, and especially in urban areas, *tú* (or *vos*) has come to be the standard choice, with *usted* used in a minority of cases to express courtesy or respect. In French, too, the use of *tu* is expanding at the expense of *vous*, but *vous* continues to be used in many situations, even between speakers who are well acquainted. The factors involved in choosing a form of address include speakers' age, gender, social status, and education, as well as the context in which the interaction takes place. Given this complexity, usage in a specific place can be learned only by observing how people there address one another.

## Detalles/Détails

The progressive loss of *ustedes* and generalized use of *vosotros* in Spain will eventually bring European Spanish into line with American Spanish and with French, where there is a formal/informal distinction in the singular but not in the plural. (This pattern can be seen in other Romance languages as well.) In one-on-one situations, speakers can choose how to address hearers; as numbers increase, however, it becomes harder to distinguish the members of a group as individuals, and so to make a formal/informal distinction.

## Suggestions for further practice

1. Watch a scene from a film in French or Spanish with English subtitles and the sound turned off. See if you can determine whether the characters are addressing each other formally (i.e., with *vous* or *usted/ustedes*) or informally (i.e., with *tu*, *tú/vos*). Then watch again with the sound on to see if you were right.
2. Search online for the rules of a sport or a board game in French or Spanish (wikiHow is a good source: fr.wikihow.com, es.wikihow.com). Identify the relative pronouns and observe how they are used.

# *Chapter 4*

## ¿CÓMO SE CONJUGAN Y SE INTERPRETAN LOS VERBOS? COMMENT SE CONJUGUENT ET S'INTERPRÈTENT LES VERBES?

Comparar/Comparer

In the Parallel Texts section at the end of the book, read *Mundial 2014/Mondial 2014* in the language you know and then compare the other language. The differences in the verbs will be explained in this chapter.

### 4A. CONJUGATION

Both languages have complicated verb systems, with multiple verb endings that vary according to the factors discussed in the following sections. Being able to produce all of these forms comes only with practice, but it is reassuring to know that there are reliable patterns. There are charts of the most common verb patterns in the appendix, and the discussion to follow highlights important details. For more patterns, consult the appendix of any good dictionary or look up a specific verb online.

Verbs in Spanish and French are divided into categories according to how they are conjugated. In both languages, there is one category that is much larger and more regular than the others: verbs whose infinitive ends in *-ar* in Spanish and in *-er* in French. New verbs—borrowed from other languages or invented because of new realities—are usually added to these categories.

 **4.1** Ejercicio/Exercice

Look at these verbs borrowed or coined for computer language: they belong to the categories *-ar* in Spanish and *-er* in French. (As often happens with borrowed words, there is more than one way to spell some of them.) Pronounce these words and then listen to see if your pronunciation was correct.

| | |
|---|---|
| *bloguear* | *bloguer* |
| *chatear* | *tchatter/chatter* |
| *descargar* | *télécharger* |
| *guglear/googlear* | *googler* |

**The verb endings of Spanish and French look more similar than they sound.** The fact that most final consonants are not pronounced in French (see chapter 1B) makes many person/number endings inaudible. Look at and listen to the present tense of the regular verb *parler* below. All of the underlined verbs have the same pronunciation. And, when speakers replace *nous* with *on* (third-person singular), which is very common in casual speech, five of the forms sound the same. This has important repercussions for the use of subject pronouns in French, as discussed in chapter 3A.

| | |
|---|---|
| *je <u>parle</u>* | *nous parlons* |
| *tu <u>parles</u>* | *vous parlez* |
| *il <u>parle</u>* | *ils <u>parlent</u>* |

When the regular verb *hablar* is conjugated in Spanish, the endings are audible—though subject pronouns may be necessary because the verb forms used in formal address are third person (see chapter 3A).

| | |
|---|---|
| *(yo) hablo* | *(nosotros/-as) hablamos* |
| *(tú) hablas* | *(vosotros/-as) habláis* **(European Spanish only)** |
| *(él/usted) habla* | *(ellos/ustedes) hablan* |

## 4B. TENSE: TIMEFRAME OF EVENTS

French and Spanish inherited the past/present/future distinction from Latin, which had simple (one-word) verbs in each of these categories.

As the languages developed, they acquired new compound (two-word) verbs, made by combining an AUXILIARY with the INFINITIVE, PARTI-CIPLE, or GERUND. The combinations of auxiliary + participle are called "**perfect**" forms, and there is one of them for each tense: present perfect (perfected, i.e., completed, with respect to the present), past perfect (completed with respect to the past), and future perfect (completed with respect to the future).

The compound perfect forms had to fit into an established verb system; they either replaced existing forms (as the past perfect and the future perfect did) or were used differently from existing forms (as the present perfect was). **French and Spanish differ in how the present-perfect form is used.**

### 4C. ASPECT: PERSPECTIVE ON EVENTS

**Tense has to do with where events are placed on the timeline. ASPECT is a separate category of verbal meaning; it has to do with how situations are perceived, regardless of when they occur.**

**Spanish and French have two sets of aspectual contrasts, in the future tense and in the past tense.** In the future, both languages have a one-word form made up of the infinitive plus endings (comparable to the *will* future in English).

*Te llamaré antes del partido. ~ Je t'appellerai avant le match.*

In addition, both languages have a compound form made up of the verb *ir/aller* plus infinitive (comparable to the *going to* future in English). Note that the Spanish conjugation has the preposition *a* between the two parts of the verb.

*Me parece que va a llover. ~ Il me semble qu'il va pleuvoir.*

Both of these verb forms refer to the future, so the difference between them cannot be explained in terms of tense; instead, the contrast is between two perspectives on future events. The one-word future (like the *will* future in English) is used to talk about events, like the promised phone call, that exist entirely in the future. In contrast, the compound future (like the *going to* future in English) refers to events, like the approaching rainstorm, that have begun in the present and continue into the future. In the many cases where this distinction is not clear, the compound future is used—which means that it is much more common.

### Comparar/Comparer

To talk about the past, French and Spanish have three conjugations that look similar: *imperfecto/imparfait*, *pretérito/passé simple*, and *presente perfecto/passé composé*. Look at these verb forms in the verb charts. The imperfect verbs share both form and function; the others are alike in form but different in function.

**Spanish and French also share two perspectives on the past.** Both languages can focus on a situation as a completed whole (perfective aspect), or ignore its limits (imperfective aspect). The imperfect verb forms are used when the limits of a situation are unknown or unimportant. The imperfect is used to talk about youth, as in the examples below, because this period of time does not have a definite beginning or end.

*Cuando yo era joven . . . ~ Quand j'étais jeune . . .*

The imperfect is also used when the beginning and end of situations are of no importance in a given context, as in the case of background events in a narrative.

*Buscaba mi asiento cuando el delantero marcó el primer gol. ~ Je cherchais ma place quand l'attaquant a marqué le premier but.*

The use of the imperfect doesn't necessarily mean that a situation has no end. In the sentences above, the imperfect aspect of *buscaba/je cherchais* means that the activity was going on when *marcó/a marqué* happened; the past TENSE means that it is over. The imperfect forms in French and Spanish share both form and function, and are easily learned.

To refer to past tense situations as completed wholes, French and Spanish use parallel forms, but in different ways. In Spanish, the present perfect and the preterit have similar meanings: completed with respect to the present vs. completed in the past, respectively. Both forms are part of the Spanish verb system, though usage varies by dialect. In much of Spain, the present perfect is used as a preterit, as the cognate form is in French. It can be used to talk about completed events, whether in the recent past or the distant past.

*Esta mañana he visto los resultados del campeonato. (Ce matin j'ai vu les résultats du championnat.)*
*He nacido en Madrid. (Je suis né/née à Madrid.)*

In Latin American Spanish (except for some Andean varieties), speakers would be more likely to say *Esta mañana vi los resultados del campeonato* and *Nací en Madrid*.

In French, the choice between the two forms depends on whether the language is used for speaking or writing and, further, on the degree of formality of the written language. **French uses the compound past** (*passé composé*) **in speaking and informal writing, and the simple past** (*passé simple*) **in formal writing.** In order to read French, you need to be able to recognize the simple past—which is easy when you know Spanish, as the forms are cognate with the Spanish preterit.

SPANISH PRESENT PERFECT
*he (has, etc.) jugado*
SPANISH PRETERIT
*jugué (jugaste, etc.)*

FRENCH COMPOUND PAST
*j'ai (tu as, etc.) joué*
FRENCH SIMPLE PAST
*je jouai (tu jouas, etc.)*

Here, French has one spoken form where Spanish has two. The compound past in French incorporates both of the meanings that can be encoded separately in Spanish; it functions as a simple preterit in some contexts, and as a present perfect in others.

**4.2** Ejercicio/Exercice

The simple past is slowly disappearing from French, even in writing; today it is unlikely to appear in e-mail messages, personal letters, or newspaper articles about popular topics. In traditional literature, though, it is used for narration. Read *Le berger menteur* (in Parallel Texts) and observe that it appears everywhere, except in dialogue.

There is an additional detail to be learned about the compound past (and the other perfect verb forms) in French: there are two auxiliary verbs that combine with the past participle. *Avoir* combines with the participle of transitive verbs (and also with *être*), and *être* with the participle of intransitive and reflexive verbs.

*Il l'a arrangé /choisi/fait/reçu. (Él lo arregló/eligió/hizo/recibió.)* vs. *Il est arrivé/né/parti/venu. (Él llegó/nació/partió/vino.)*

With *être*, the participle functions as an adjective and must agree with the subject in gender and number. For example, if the subject of the sentence above is *elle*, the participle becomes *arrivée/née/partie/venue*; if the subject is *ils*, the participle becomes *arrivés/nés/partis/venus*.

## 4.3 Ejercicio/Exercice

In the sentences below (adapted from the parallel text *Mondial 2014*), the participles should agree with the subjects because the auxiliary is *être*. What is the correct form of the participle in each case?

*Les spectateurs ont <u>suivi</u> la finale.* _____
*L'équipe allemande est <u>devenu</u> championne du monde.* _____
*Deux cent mille Argentins sont <u>venu</u>.* _____
*Beaucoup de personnes se sont <u>rassemblé</u>.* _____

**Spanish uses only one auxiliary verb to form the perfect tenses:** *haber*. In these compound verbs, the participle is invariable; it has only one form, ending in *-o*. When combined with *ser* and *estar*, though, the participle acts as an adjective and—like all adjectives—reflects the gender and number of the noun it modifies (see section 3F below).

Detalles/Détails

Historically, Spanish and English were once like French in having two auxiliaries that were used to form the perfect tenses; in both cases, only one verb remains in the modern language: *haber* in Spanish and *have* in English. (You can see sentences like *I am come* in nineteenth-century English novels.) French, too, might eventually develop in this way, because *avoir* is far and away the most common auxiliary. When children are learning French, they use only *avoir*, and there are dialects of French in which only this auxiliary is used in the spoken language.

**4.4** Ejercicio/Exercice

This short text is written in the *passé composé*. Predict which auxiliary will be used with each participle.

*Je _____ tombée amoureuse du football quand j'_____*
   *(suis/ai)*     *(suis/ai)*
*assisté avec mon père au match d'ouverture du Mondial en 1998.*
*Nous _____ arrivés très tôt et il m'_____ acheté un*
   *(sommes/avons)*     *(est/a)*
*maillot officiel de l'équipe de France que j'_____ tout de*
    *(suis/ai)*
*suite mis.*

*tomber amoureux = enamorarse, assister = asistir, arriver = llegar,*
*acheter = comprar, mettre = ponerse*

Detalles/Détails

Some verbs—*descendre, monter, entrer, rentrer, sortir, passer,* and *retourner*—appear to combine with either auxiliary, *être* or *avoir*, in the compound past. The Spanish translations show, however, that in each case there are actually two different verbs with the same name: one transitive and one intransitive.

*Il a rentré la poubelle.* ~ *Él guardó/ha guardado el cubo de la basura.*
  **vs.** *Il est rentré chez lui.* ~ *Él volvió/ha vuelto a casa.*
*Elle a sorti l'argent de son compte.* ~ *Ella sacó/ha sacado el dinero de su*
  *cuenta.* **vs.** *Elle est sortie à trois heures.* ~ *Ella salió/ha salido a las*
  *tre.*

## 4D. MOOD: EVALUATION OF EVENTS

Comparar/Comparer
*Me es igual. Haz lo que <u>quieras</u>.* (subjunctive) vs. *Ça m'est égal. Fais ce que tu <u>veux</u>.* (indicative)

In Spanish and French, the indicative/subjunctive contrast is used to evaluate information. In subordinate clauses, the subjunctive marks information that is considered unreliable (because it is doubtful or unreal) or uninformative (because it is already known). Usage is similar in the two languages. **In Spanish, however, there are more subjunctive verb forms, and the subjunctive is required in a wider range of cases than in French.**

### Subjunctive verb forms

In both languages, the subjunctive forms are made by adding endings to indicative stems (i.e., the verb minus person/number endings)— which means that any irregularities in the stems will appear in the subjunctive as well. Spanish has (1) a present subjunctive based on the stem of the first person singular (*yo*) form of the present tense, to which -*e* is added for -*ar* verbs and -*a* for -*er* and -*ir* verbs; (2) two past subjunctives based on the stem of the third-person-plural (*ellos*) form of the preterit, one with -*ra* added to the stem and one with -*se*; and (3) two compound subjunctives made up of the present and the past subjunctive of *haber* plus the participle. All of these forms are used in contemporary Spanish, though the past subjunctive with -*se* is slowly losing ground and can be learned for recognition only. (The *-se* forms are included in the verb chart but do not appear in the examples below.)

---

**4.5** Ejercicio/Exercice

Observe how the subjunctive forms of these Spanish verbs are derived. The stem of the base form is underlined.

| | | | |
|---|---|---|---|
| *LLEGAR* | present subjunctive based on <u>LLEG</u>O (+ orthographic *u*, added to separate *g* from *e*) + *e* + person/number endings | = | *llegue, llegues, llegue, lleguemos, (lleguéis), lleguen* |
| | past subjunctive based on <u>LLEGA</u>RON + *ra* + person/number endings | = | *llegara, llegaras, llegara, llegáramos, (llegarais), llegaran* |
| *TENER* | present subjunctive based on <u>TENG</u>O + *a* + person/number endings | = | *tenga, tengas, tenga, tengamos, (tengáis), tengan* |
| | past subjunctive based on <u>TUVIE</u>RON + *ra* + person/number endings | = | *tuviera, tuvieras, tuviera, tuviéramos, (tuvierais), tuvieran* |
| *SERVIR* | present subjunctive based on <u>SIRV</u>O + *a* + person/number endings | = | *sirva, sirvas, sirva, sirvamos, (sirváis), sirvan* |
| | past subjunctive based on <u>SIRVIE</u>RON + *ra* + person/number endings | = | *sirviera, sirvieras, sirviera, sirviéramos, (sirvierais), sirvieran* |

---

Detalles/Détails

It is common in Spanish—but not in French—for the subject to follow the verb in subordinate clauses. As you go through this section, observe the word order in the subordinate clauses of the example sentences.

Since there are numerous subjunctive forms in Spanish, you need to know which one to use. There are two "sequence of tenses" rules that work most of the time. If the main clause is in the present or the future, use the present subjunctive in the subordinate clause:

*No quiero que pierda el equipo nacional.*

If the main clause is in the past, use the past subjunctive:

*No quería que perdiera el equipo nacional.*

In languages that are both spoken and written, there are always words and constructions that are used in writing but not in speech (and vice versa). **In spoken French, there are only two forms of the subjunctive.** The "present" subjunctive of regular verbs is based on the common stem of the third-person-plural (*ils*) and the first-person-plural (*nous*) forms of the present tense, to which -*e* is added for the *je*, *tu*, *il*, and *ils* forms or -*i* for the *nous* and *vous* forms, followed by the person/number endings. **This means that the present subjunctive of regular -*er* verbs differs from the present indicative only in the *nous* and *vous* forms** (and remember that *nous* can be replaced by third-person-singular *on*). In Spanish, because the "opposite vowel" (-*e* for -*ar* verbs, -*a* for -*er* and -*ir* verbs) is used to form the present subjunctive, those forms are unambiguously distinct from the indicative.

For a minority of French verbs (like *boire* below), *ils* and *nous* have different stems in the present indicative, so there are two base forms: the *ils* stem for the *je*, *tu*, *il*, *ils* subjunctive forms, and the *nous* stem for the *nous* and *vous* subjunctive forms. Compare this with Spanish, where a single base form—regular or irregular—applies throughout the subjunctive conjugations.

**4.6** Ejercicio/Exercice

Observe how the present subjunctive of these French verbs is formed. The roots of the base forms are underlined.

| | | | |
|---|---|---|---|
| *AIMER* | based on *AIMENT/ AIMONS* + *e* (*je, tu, il, ils*) or *i* (*nous, vous*) + person/number endings | = | *j'aime, tu aimes, il/elle/ on aime, nous aimions, vous aimiez, ils/elles aiment* |
| *FINIR* | based on *FINISSENT/ FINISSONS* + *e* (*je, tu, il, ils*) or *i* (*nous, vous*) + person/number endings | = | *je finisse, tu finisses, il/ elle/on finisse, nous finissions, vous finissiez, ils/elles finissent* |
| *BOIRE* | based on *BOIVENT* + *e* (*je, tu, il, ils*) and *BUVONS* + *i* (*nous, vous*) + person/number endings | = | *je boive, tu boives, il/ elle/on boive, nous buvions, vous buviez, ils/elles boivent* |

The French "past" subjunctive is a compound verb made up of the present subjunctive of *avoir* or *être* plus the participle. The words "present" and "past" appear in quotes because usage of the forms does not correspond to present and past tense. There are also two verb forms that appear only in very formal writing: a one-word past subjunctive that takes its root from the *passé simple*, a form that itself appears only in writing (see section 3C above); and a pluperfect subjunctive, made up of the past imperfect of *avoir* or *être* plus the participle. These two literary subjunctives are not part of the spoken language but are listed in dictionaries and reference grammars.

Now look at the sentences in French that correspond to the previous examples in Spanish. The same subjunctive verb is used in both; in other words, the French "present" subjunctive can be used in past-tense contexts.

*Je ne veux pas que l'équipe nationale perde.* ~ *No quiero que pierda el equipo nacional.*

*Je ne voulais pas que l'équipe nationale perde.* ~ *No quería que perdiera el equipo nacional.*

Of course, it is always possible to react in the present to something in the past, which results in a mix of tenses.

*C'est formidable que l'équipe nationale <u>ait gagné</u>. ~ Es fantástico que <u>ganara</u>/<u>haya ganado</u> el equipo nacional.*

The subjunctive is not used in the sentences above to mark unreal information—quite the contrary. Here the victory of the national team is not a hoped-for event, but an accomplished fact. In both languages, the subjunctive is used in subordinate clauses to mark information that is redundant, that is, known to speaker and hearer, in contrast with a reaction/comment (often called "emotion") in the main clause. Notice that the past subjunctive appears in the French sentence above although the main clause is in the present tense; it is used because the time of the subordinate clause is prior to that of the main clause. This chronology—subordinate clause prior to main clause—also cues the past subjunctive when the main clause is in the past tense.

*J'étais déçu que l'équipe nationale n'<u>ait</u> pas <u>gagné</u>. ~ Estaba decepcionado de que no <u>ganara</u> el equipo nacional.*

### The subjunctive and unknown/unreal information
Both Spanish and French use the subjunctive after conjunctions like *antes de que*/*avant que* and *para que*/*pour que*, which introduce subordinate clauses that are in the future with respect to the main clause (whether that clause is in the present or the past tense).

*Me fui antes de que <u>llegaras</u>* (past subj.) *al partido. ~ Je suis parti avant que tu <u>arrives</u>* (pres. subj.) *au match.*

There is also a temporal gap after an expression of obligation (necessity, etc.) or commanding (hoping, preferring, wishing, recommending, etc.). The fulfillment of the obligation or command will always be subsequent in time.

*Es necesario que el entrenador <u>sea</u> exigente. ~ Il faut que l'entraîneur*
*<u>soit</u> exigeant.*

*Querían que el equipo <u>jugara</u>* (past subj.) *al nivel nacional. ~ Ils vou-*
*laient que l'équipe <u>joue</u>* (pres. subj.) *au niveau national.*

## Detalles/Détails

The present subjunctive *arrives* and *joue* in the preceding examples are
identical to the present indicative forms. There is overlap between the
present indicative and the present subjunctive of regular *-er* verbs for
all forms except *nous* and *vous*. The *nous* and *vous* forms are subjunctive *arrivions/jouions* and *arriviez/jouiez* vs. indicative *arrivons/jouons*
and *arrivez/jouez*. (But, the distinctive *nous* and *vous* subjunctive forms
are in most cases the same as the corresponding imperfect indicative
forms! You can see all of this in the verb charts at the end of this book.)

**Spanish is consistent in requiring the subjunctive when the subor-
dinate clause has not yet happened at the time of the main clause,
whether present or past.** There is no future subjunctive (in either language), so the present subjunctive is understood to refer to the future.
**French, in contrast, uses the future indicative in some of these cases.**

*Espero que el portero <u>llegue</u>* (pres. subj.) *a tiempo. ~ J'espère que le*
*gardien <u>arrivera</u>* (fut. indic.) *à temps.*

When referring to future time after *cuando/quand*, the subjunctive is
used in Spanish, but the future indicative is used in French.

*Cuando <u>termine/haya terminado</u>* (pres./pres. perfect subj.) *el partido*
*te vendré a buscar. ~ Quand le match <u>finira/aura fini</u>* (fut./fut.
perfect indic.) *je viendrai te chercher.*

When the latter sentence is cast in the past tense in Spanish, both verbs
move to the parallel past form: past subjunctive and conditional. The
same thing happens in French, resulting in conditional/conditional
perfect and conditional.

*Te dije que cuando* <u>*terminaras*</u> (past subj.) *te vendría a buscar.* ~ *Je t'ai dit que quand tu* <u>*finirais/aurais fini*</u> (cond. /cond. perfect indic.) *je viendrais te chercher.*

Sometimes, the main clause overtly states that the information in the subordinate clause is not reliable, for example, *Dudo, Es posible/ Je doute, C'est possible.* Both Spanish and French use the subjunctive in the subordinate clause of such sentences, but there is one case where the two languages are not parallel:

*Es probable que él* <u>*venga*</u> (pres. subj.) *mañana.* ~ *C'est probable qu'il* <u>*viendra*</u> (fut. indic.) *demain.*

### Detalles/Détails

Although the compound future (*aller* + infinitive) is much more common, it is the simple form of the future that is required in the preceding French sentences. In Spanish, too, the simple future has some uses that shade into conjecture (e.g., *Serán las dos* = *It must be two o'clock*).

### 4.7 Ejercicio/Exercice

In the French version of this e-mail message, the underlined verbs are in the indicative. Fill in the blanks in the Spanish version, where the equivalent verbs must be in the subjunctive.

*Merci pour l'invitation à ce match formidable. J'espère que tu* <u>*as pu*</u> *te reposer le lendemain. Il est probable que je* <u>*reviendrai*</u> *en automne. Je t'appellerai quand mes projets* <u>*seront*</u> *finalisés.*
*Gracias por la invitación a ese magnífico partido. Espero que _____ (poder) descansar al día siguiente. Es probable que _____ (volver) en el otoño. Te llamaré cuando _____ (estar) finalizados mis planes.*

**Subjunctive and indicative after** *si/si*

When there is a cause-effect relationship between the two parts of a sentence, *si/si* is used to introduce the potential cause. The indicative is used in cause-effect sentences.

*Si puedo, te invitaré.* ~ *Si je peux, je t'inviterai.*

In CONTRARY-TO-FACT sentences, the cause does not exist, and, therefore, there can be no effect. In Spanish, the past subjunctive is used after *si* to mark contrary-to-fact information, and the conditional is used in the other clause. In contrary-to-fact sentences in French, the imperfect indicative is used in the *si* clause.

*Si pudiera, te invitaría.* ~ *Si je pouvais, je t'inviterais.*

Both languages use the past tense in the *si/si* clause of contrary-to-fact sentences—Spanish in the subjunctive, and French in the indicative—though the reference is not to past time. To refer to past time in a contrary-to-fact sentence, compound forms are used:

*Si hubiera podido, te habría invitado.* ~ *Si j'avais pu, je t'aurais invité(e).*

Detalles/Détails

Contrary-to-fact sentences are complex in both form and meaning, and speakers often simplify them. There are many simplifications in Spanish; one of them involves using the infinitive after *de* rather than conjugating the verb: *Si yo fuera tú* → *De ser tú*. Some French speakers are now using the conditional in both clauses without *si*: *Je serais toi, j'irais.*

**4.8** Ejercicio/Exercice

Match the sayings to one another. As you do so, look at the verb forms used after *si/si* and classify the sentences as cause-effect or contrary-to-fact.

| | |
|---|---|
| *Si nada arriesgas, nada tendrás.* | *Si Dieu n'existait pas, il faudrait l'inventer.* |
| *Si dices las verdades, pierdes las amistades.* | *Si la mer était du vin, tout le monde serait marin.* |
| *Si la mar fuera vino, todo el mundo sería marino.* | *Si on dit la vérité, on perd l'amitié.* |
| *Si Dios no existiera, habría que inventarlo.* | *Si tu ne risques rien, tu n'auras rien.* |

Over time, the subjunctive in French has been reduced to fewer forms. You can see in the verb charts at the end of this book that many subjunctive forms are the same as indicative forms—and even forms that have different spellings may have the same pronunciation. The subjunctive appears automatically in certain sentences; there are only a few cases in French in which there is a choice between subjunctive and indicative—and in these cases the option is available in Spanish as well.

*Je ne crois pas qu'elle soit/est gagnante.* ~ *No creo que ella sea/es la ganadora.* *C'est le match le plus impressionnant qu'on ait/a jamais vu.* ~ *Es el partido más impresionante que se haya/ha visto jamás.*

**In Spanish, the subjunctive is much more robust than in French.** There are many forms and most of them are used regularly. And, though most subjunctive usage is governed by grammatical rules, there are many contexts in which speakers have to decide whether to use indicative or subjunctive. The sentences below show a few of these contexts.

*Lo haré como/cuando/donde me dicen.* (how/when/where) vs. *Lo haré como/cuando/donde me digan.* (however/whenever/wherever)

**Going from French to Spanish, you have to learn to master a wider range of forms and extend your use of the subjunctive to a wider range of cases. Going from Spanish to French, you have to learn not to match tenses and not to use the subjunctive in some places where it is required in Spanish.**

## 4E. VOICE: CAUSATION OF EVENTS

In grammar, the word *subject* has a meaning similar to its general meaning: the subject of a sentence is what the sentence is about, just as the subject of an essay is what the essay is about. In "active" sentences, subjects play the role of agents, that is, they perform actions.

*Siete países establecieron la FIFA. ~ Sept pays ont établi la FIFA.*

Of course, the agent does not have to be the subject of the sentence. In "passive" sentences, the agent appears in a prepositional phrase, and the former direct object becomes the grammatical subject and the topic of the sentence.

*La FIFA fue establecida por siete países. ~ La FIFA a été établie par sept pays.*

The agent can also be left out completely.

*La FIFA fue establecida en 1904. ~ La FIFA a été établie en 1904.*
(*fut établie* in formal writing, as in promotional materials)

There are other structures, too, that allow events to be talked about without specifying the agent. One option is to put the pronoun *se/se* in place of the agent.

*La FIFA se estableció en 1904. ~ La FIFA s'est établie en 1904.*

These last two sentences look reflexive (see chapter 3D), but they are not. FIFA did not establish itself, of course; rather, because the pronoun *se/se* is neutral for person and number, it can stand in for an unnamed agent.

In Spanish, a third-person-plural verb without a specified subject is understood to be impersonal as well.

*Establecieron la FIFA en 1904.*

This option is not available in French, because subject pronouns must always appear with conjugated verbs (see chapter 4A). Instead, French makes use of impersonal *on*.

*On a établi la FIFA en 1904.*

This is the most common way to avoid identifying the agent in French; the parallel use of *uno* in Spanish is much more restricted.

### 4F. *SER* AND *ESTAR* IN SPANISH

Comparar/Comparer
*A veces el pastorcito se aburría de estar solo en el campo.* **vs.** *Parfois le petit berger s'ennuyait d'être seul dans la campagne.* (from Parallel Texts)

Speakers of French have to learn how to distinguish the two COPULAS (verbs used to link one part of a sentence with another) in Spanish. Where French has only *être*, Spanish has *ser* and *estar*. That both verbs can have the same translation in French does **not** mean that they are interchangeable in Spanish; *ser* and *estar* are used in different ways.

Only *ser* is used to link a noun or pronoun with the subject of a sentence.

*El portugués es el delantero.* ~ *Le Portugais est l'attaquant.*

*Estar* is usually used to locate the subject.

*Mi casa está cerca del estadio.* ~ *Ma maison est près du stade.*

When a location is treated as a noun, however, *ser* is used. In the sentences below, the pronouns *esta/celle-ci* can replace *aquí/ici*, which makes it clear that the latter function like nouns.

*Mi casa es aquí (es esta).* ~ *Ma maison est ici (est celle-ci).*

Only *estar* is used with the gerund, as part of the "progressive" (i.e., action in progress) form of the verb. In both languages, the simple present tense can be used with progressive meaning as well.

*Estoy mirando (miro) el partido.* ~ *Je suis en train de regarder (je regarde) le match.*

With adjectives, either verb can be used, with a contrast in meaning. With *ser*, the adjective names a characteristic (i.e., a defining feature); with *estar*, the adjective names a state (i.e., an incidental feature). This contrast can be expressed in French, of course, but not with the copula.

*El delantero es agresivo.* (**characteristically**) ~ *L'attaquant est agressif.* vs. *El delantero está agresivo.* (**circumstantially**) ~ *L'attaquant se montre agressif.*

Time and place are the defining characteristics of events, so *ser* links events with the time and place where they occur.

*El partido es a las ocho en el estadio.* ~ *Le match est à huit heures au stade.*

With the participle, either verb can be used. When *ser* is combined with the participle of an action verb, the result is the passive voice, that is, reference is to an action. When *estar* is combined with the participle, reference is to a state (the result of a prior action).

*El estadio fue construido en 2004.* ~ *Le stade a été construit en 2004.* (*fut construit* in formal writing, as on a dedicatory plaque) *El estadio está mal construido.* ~ *Le stade est mal construit.*

---

**4.9** Ejercicio/Exercice

Read these sentences from the interview in French with Salvador Dali (in Parallel Texts) and decide whether the underlined verbs should be *ser* or *estar* in Spanish.

*Vous-même, vous vous trouvez intelligent?*

SD: *Je <u>suis</u> un monstre d'intelligence.*  soy/estoy

*Vous regrettez d'<u>être</u> intelligent?*  ser/estar

SD: *Je le regrette pour ma peinture.*

*Que pensez-vous des gens qui collectionnent vos tableaux?*

SD: *Ce <u>sont</u> des gens qui ont un très grand sens*  son/están
*pratique.*

*Comment supportez-vous la solitude?*

SD: *Je ne <u>suis</u> jamais seul.*  soy/estoy

*J'ai l'habitude d'<u>être</u> toujours avec Salvador Dali.*  ser/estar

---

**Suggestions for further practice**

1. Choose a historical event and look up the French and Spanish Wikipedia entries for it. Compare the tenses used.

2. Start a collection of proverbs, sayings, or famous quotations that you like in French or Spanish and commit a few to memory.

# Chapter 5

## ¿COMO SE ESTRUCTURAN LAS FRASES? COMMENT SE STRUCTURENT LES PHRASES?

### 5A. QUESTIONS

Comparar/Comparer
Look at the *entrevista/interview* with Salvador Dali (in Parallel Texts) and observe how questions are asked in the two languages.

**Yes-no questions**
**There are more question patterns in French than in Spanish.** The Spanish pattern is quite simple: in yes-no questions, the subject is placed after the verb. Subject pronouns are infrequently used, however, so the primary difference is intonation, with rising intonation signaling a question. Since intonation cannot be seen on the page, the orthographic symbol ¿ signals that a question follows.

*¿Quiere usted facturar una maleta?*

This question can be answered either *sí* or *no*.
In French, there are many patterns for yes-no questions. The simplest option, used in informal speech, is to use intonation alone. Another common pattern is to begin the question with the question marker *est-ce que*, which is like a lexical equivalent of ¿ in Spanish. A slightly more complex option is to invert the subject-verb order; the inversion is spelled with a hyphen between the verb and the subject.

*Vous voulez enregistrer une valise?*
*Est-ce que vous voulez enregistrer une valise?*
*Voulez-vous enregistrer une valise?*

These questions can be answered either *oui* or *non*. But an affirmative answer to a negative question begins with *si*, not with *oui*: *Vous n'allez pas enregistrer votre valise?* → *Si, je vais l'enregistrer*. In Spanish, *sí* is usually repeated in the affirmative answer to a negative question: *¿No va a facturar su maleta?* → *Sí, sí la voy a facturar*.

## Detalles/Détails

When the subject and verb are inverted in French, the consonant at the end of the verb may be pronounced because of liaison (chapter 1B). Here are some examples, with the pronounced consonant underlined:

| | |
|---|---|
| *Peut-on faire une réservation en ligne?* | *(¿Se puede hacer una reservación en línea?)* |
| *Est-elle arrivée en retard?* | *(¿Llegó tarde?)* |
| *Ont-ils réservé leurs billets?* | *(¿Reservaron sus billetes?)* |
| *Le train sort-il à midi?* | *(¿Sale el tren a mediodia?)* |
| *L'agent parle-t-il français?* | *(¿Habla francés el agente?)* |
| *Quand va-t-elle partir?* | *(¿Cuándo va a salir?)* |

In the last two examples, note that *t* is added in inverted questions between a verb ending in a vowel followed by a subject pronoun beginning with a vowel.

**Interrogative-word questions**
**Again, there are more options in French. In Spanish, interrogative words (all of which carry a written accent) appear before the verb.**

*¿Dónde/cómo/cuándo/con quién/por qué viaja usted?*

In French, if the question begins with a question word, either the interrogation marker *est-ce que* is used, or the subject follows the verb.

*Où/comment/quand/avec qui/pourquoi est-ce que vous voyagez?*
*Où/comment/quand/avec qui/pourquoi voyagez-vous?*

These questions sound formal and are used in writing and in conventional expressions such as *Comment allez-vous?* The most common informal pattern simply puts the question word at the end. (Notice that here, as usual, the informal option is also the simplest.)

*Vous voyagez où/comment/quand/avec qui/pourquoi?*

In French, the answer to *pourquoi* is *parce que*, but in Spanish the answer to *por qué* is *porque* (all one word, no accent mark).

Detalles/Détails
The title of this chapter could be rendered in a number of additional ways in French, including:

*Comment est-ce qu'on structure les phrases?*
*Comment est-ce que les phrases se structurent?*
*Comment les phrases se structurent-elles?*
*Comment structure-t-on les phrases?*

The number of options in Spanish is more limited because: (1) although *¿Es que . . . ?* is a possible way of asking questions in Spanish, it is not lexicalized as a question marker, and (2) the subject pronoun *ellas* cannot take the place of a nonhuman noun like *frases*.

**5.1 Ejercicio/Exercice**

Supply one question for each of the Spanish answers below, and two questions (i.e., two forms of the same question) for each of the French answers.

*Estoy en el aeropuerto.*     *Sale mañana (ella).*
*Je suis à l'aéroport.*     *Elle part demain.*
*Sí, lo tengo (el pasaporte).*     *No, no viajan con ellos (los niños).*
*Oui, je l'ai (le passeport).*     *Non, ils ne voyagent pas avec eux (les enfants).*

## 5B. NEGATION

**The negative words in Spanish are easy to identify because they begin with *n*.**

*no*
*nada* (both an adverb, as below, and a pronoun)
*nadie*
*ninguno/-a* (both an adjective, as below, and a pronoun)
*nunca* (less frequently *jamás*, which may be combined with *nunca* to
   produce *nunca jamás/jamás nunca* = *plus jamais/jamais plus*)

The general rule is that a negative word must precede the verb.

*El agente no ayuda.*

*No* is used in combination with other negative words, which produces multiple negation.

*El agente no ayuda nada, en ninguna parte, nunca, a nadie.*

If another negative word is placed before the verb, then *no* is not used.

*Nadie ayuda nunca en ninguna parte.*

**In French, there is a formal/written pattern for negation and an informal/spoken one.** In the formal pattern, negation both precedes and follows the verb.

*ne . . . pas*
*ne . . . rien* (adverb), *rien ne . . .* (pronoun)
*ne . . . personne* (adverb), *personne ne . . .* (pronoun)
*ne . . . aucun/aucune* (adjective and pronoun, e.g., *aucun de mes amis
   ne . . .*)

*ne . . . nulle part (en ninguna parte)*
*ne . . . jamais*
*ne . . . plus*
*ne . . . pas encore (todavía no)*

As in Spanish, multiple negation is possible.

*Il n'aide plus jamais personne.*

In spoken French, it is common to eliminate *ne*, leaving only the second half of the formula. Putting the negative after the verb leaves the subject and verb together, thus maintaining the tight bond between these two parts of the sentence in French.

*Je sais/veux pas. ~ No sé/quiero.*

## 5.2 Ejercicio/Exercice

On the left are some common expressions in French in which *ne* is not used. Match them with the equivalent expressions in Spanish, taking note of the differences.

| | |
|---|---|
| *Ça marche pas.* | *No puedo más.* |
| *C'est pas vrai/possible/ nécessaire.* | *No tenemos nada más que decir.* |
| *Ça fait rien.* | *No hay más.* |
| *J'en peux plus.* | *No funciona.* |
| *J'ai pas le choix.* | *No tengo otra opción.* |
| *J'ai aucune idée.* | *No es verdad/posible/necesario.* |
| *On a plus rien à dire.* | *No pasa nada.* |
| *Il y en a plus.*† | *No tengo (ninguna) idea.* |

†Since the word *plus* means *más*, this expression is ambiguous without *ne*: it could mean either *there's more* or *there's no more*. In order to resolve the ambiguity, speakers pronounce the *-s* in *plus* with affirmative meaning.

Detalles/Détails

The words *pas, plus,* and *personne (paso, más, persona)* function as negatives in French, though their meaning is not inherently negative. In Spanish, a similar process has taken place with the phrases *en mi vida,* often used instead of *nunca en mi vida (jamais de la vie),* and *en absoluto,* instead of *no . . . en absoluto (ne . . . pas du tout).*

## 5C. COMMANDS

Comparar/Comparer

*Créame, esto es una fiesta permanente.* vs. *Cela, croyez-moi, c'est une fête permanente.* (from Parallel Texts)

Except for the affirmative *tú* or *vos* forms, commands in Spanish are conjugated just like the corresponding present subjunctive verbs. Affirmative *tú* commands are the same as the present-tense indicative without the final *-s,* though a number of common verbs have a one-syllable command form (see the verb charts).

*Toma un taxi.*

Where *vos* is used instead of *tú,* the affirmative commands can be derived by removing the final *-r* from the infinitive.

*Tomá un taxi.*

The negative version of both *tú* and *vos* commands is the *tú* form of the present subjunctive.

*No tomes un taxi.*

When addressed to *usted* and *ustedes,* the verb forms for affirmative and negative commands are the same.

*Tome un taxi./No tome un taxi.*
*Tomen un taxi./No tomen un taxi.*

Object pronouns follow affirmative commands, in the order indirect-direct, and are attached to them in writing. The accent mark shows that the verb continues to be stressed despite the added syllables.

*Cómpramelo. (tú)/Comprámelo. (vos)/Cómpremelo. (Ud.)/Cómpren-melo. (Uds.)*

The object pronouns precede negative commands and are written separately.

*No me lo compres. (tú/vos)/No me lo compre. (Ud.)/No me lo compren. (Uds.)*

First-person-plural commands (*let's*) are simply the *nosotros* form of the present subjunctive. When the reflexive pronoun is added, the final -*s* is removed from the command: *Comprémonoslo (compremos + nos + lo)*. Sometimes the indicative is used as a command, as in the well-known *Vámonos*.

## Detalles/Détails

As with *tú* commands, the commands for *vosotros* (the plural of *tú* in Spain) have two forms, one affirmative and one negative (e.g., *tomad* and *no toméis*). Informally, the infinitive is used as the affirmative command, which serves to avoid a complication: the final consonant must be removed from the affirmative command when the reflexive pronoun *os* is added (*tomaos*), but not from the infinitive (*tomaros*).

Commands in French consist of the present indicative conjugations of *tu*, *vous*, and *nous*, without the pronouns. The -*s* of the *tu* form of -*er* verbs is omitted in writing. The only irregularity is that there are four verbs with commands from the present subjunctive (see the verb charts).

*Prends/prenez/prenons un taxi.*
*Ne perds/perdez/perdons pas le billet.*

In negative commands, the object pronouns (*me*, *te*, *nous*, *vous*, *le*, *la*, *les*, *lui*, *leur*, *y*, *en*) precede the verb and appear in the order described in chapter 3: *me*, *te*, *nous*, and *vous* appear first; then *le*, *la*, and *les*; then *lui* and *leur*; followed by *y* and then *en*.

> *Prends cet argent et ne me le rends pas. ~ Toma este dinero y no me lo devuelvas.*

In affirmative commands, object pronouns follow the verb and are connected to it by a hyphen. In addition, the first- and second-person singular direct and indirect objects are *moi* and *toi* (reduced to *m'* and *t'* when followed by *en*).

> *Prends-le. ~ Tómalo.*

If more than one object pronoun is used in affirmative commands, the order followed is direct object, indirect object (the opposite of the Spanish order!), *y*, *en* (connected by an apostrophe in the case of *m'en*, *t'en*).

> *Achetez-leur-en (de l'eau). ~ Cómpreles/cómprenles agua.*
> *Rends-la-lui. ~ Devuélvesela.*
> *Achète-le-moi. ~ Cómpramelo.*
> *Va-t'en! ~ ¡Vete!*

### Detalles/Détails

In order for commands to serve their communicative function, they have to be recognized as commands—and not some other verb form. In Spanish, the affirmative *tú/vos* commands are distinctive because they do not end in *-s*, like other *tú/vos* verb forms. And all the other commands are distinctive in being conjugated like the subjunctive, but not in a subordinate clause. In French, the command forms are distinctive in not having subject pronouns, which obligatorily appear with other conjugated verbs. In both languages, affirmative commands are clearly distinguished from negative commands—because it's important that the difference between them be understood.

**5.3** Ejercicio/Exercice

Match the commands on the left with their equivalent on the right. As you do this, notice the differences.

| | |
|---|---|
| *No me lo digas.* | *Explique-le-moi.* |
| *Vete.* | *Ne me le dis pas.* |
| *No te preocupes.* | *Va-t'en.* |
| *Díselo.* | *Ne leur en parle pas.* |
| *Explícamelo.* | *Ne t'inquiète pas.* |
| *No les hables de eso.* | *Dis-le-lui/leur.* |

## 5D. WORD ORDER

Word order in Spanish and French varies stylistically as well as grammatically, but it is not random in either language; on the contrary, the word-order variations discussed below are quite regular. **Word order is somewhat more variable in Spanish than in French.**

In both languages, adjectives can appear either before or after the nouns they modify, and after the noun is the most common placement.

*la Casa Blanca* ~ *la Maison Blanche*

Placing the adjective before the noun is also possible in both languages. The placement of adjectives depends on their function: if the adjective is contrastive (i.e., if it serves to distinguish one entity from others like it), then the adjective goes after the noun. And, since many adjectives serve this function, postposition is quite common. However, adjectives can appear before nouns when the noun is unique—and therefore there is no possibility of contrast.

*El Santo Padre va a visitar Paraguay.* ~ *Le Saint-Père va visiter le Paraguay.*

Adjective-noun order also occurs when the quality named by the adjective is inherent to the noun.

*¡Con el <u>refrescante</u> sabor de menta!* ~ *Avec un <u>rafraichissant</u> goût de menthe!*

Many French grammars have a list of adjectives that often appear before nouns, but in Spanish it would be impossible to compile such a list, as most adjectives can appear before the noun they modify if they do not serve a contrastive function. In both languages, there are conventionalized, slightly different meanings attached to certain adjectives depending on whether they appear before or after the noun—*un viejo amigo/un amigo viejo, un pauvre homme/un homme pauvre*, etc.—but these cases are best understood as confirmation of the generalization above.

### Detalles/Détails

In both Spanish and French, there are a few adjectives that appear in shortened form before a singular, masculine noun. This is the case with Spanish *alguno/ninguno, bueno/malo, uno/primero*, which become *algún/ningún, buen/mal, un/primer*; this produces, for example, *un buen amigo*. The same thing happens in French, in somewhat more complicated form. The adjectives *beau, nouveau* and *vieux* become *bel, nouvel* and *vieil* before singular, masculine nouns that begin with a vowel (including nouns that are spelled with an initial unpronounced *h*); this results in, for example, *un bel homme*. (There are a few other adjectives that participate in these patterns, which you can find in a reference grammar or online.)

### 5.4 Ejercicio/Exercice

In both French and Spanish, placement of the adjectives in the sentences below depends on whether or not the adjective serves a contrastive function. Decide where the adjectives should be placed and make them match the nouns they modify in gender and number.

*Conocí a tu* _____ *vecina* _____ *en el barco.*
   *(encantador)*
*Prefiero los* _____ *viajes* _____. *(organizado)*
*En París puedes ver la* _____ *Mona Lisa* _____.
   *(famoso)*
*¿Cuánto es la* _____ *tarifa* _____? *(normal)*
*Vamos a esquiar en la* _____ *cordillera* _____ *de los*
   *Andes. (magnífico)*
*Pasaremos tres días en* _____ *Edimburgo* _____.
   *(histórico)*
*J'ai rencontré ta* _____ *voisine* _____ *sur le bateau.*
   *(charmant)*
*Je préfère les* _____ *voyages* _____. *(organisé)*
*A Paris tu peux voir la* _____ *Joconde* _____. *(célèbre)*
*Quel est le* _____ *tarif* _____? *(normal)*
*On va skier dans la* _____ *Cordillère* _____ *des Andes.*
   *(magnifique)*
*Nous allons passer trois jours dans la* _____ *ville* _____
   *d'Édimbourg. (historique)*

---

In the case of subject-verb (SV) order, French and Spanish differ—though the difference is not absolute but a matter of degree. In both languages, the most common word order is SV, but in Spanish there is a strong tendency for verb-subject (VS) order in subordinate clauses.

*El billete que <u>compró mi hermana</u> es baratísimo. ~ Le billet que <u>ma soeur a acheté</u> est très bon marché.*

And, subjects also follow verbs in Spanish when they convey new information, as in the answer to a question.

*Qué aerolínea acepta animales? Creo que los <u>acepta Lufthansa.</u> ~ Quelle compagnie aérienne accepte les animaux? Je crois que <u>Lufthansa</u> les <u>accepte.</u>*

Compared with French, the greater likelihood in Spanish of using VS order in subordinate clauses and to convey new information is due to the greater ease of identifying the subject of any given verb. The audible endings on verbs and nouns make it possible to match subjects with verbs, no matter where they are placed. And, the personal *a* that marks specific, human direct objects serves to identify the subject by a process of elimination.

---

**Suggestions for further practice**

1. Watch clips from game shows in French or Spanish on YouTube or Dailymotion, paying special attention to how questions are formed.
2. Before disposing of user's manuals, packaging, instruction booklets, etc., read the French and/or Spanish and observe the use of commands and object pronouns.

## Chapter 6

# ¿CÓMO SE CLASIFICAN LAS PALABRAS? COMMENT SE CLASSIFIENT LES MOTS?

## 6A. ADVERBS

### Comparar/Comparer

*Han comido <u>copiosamente</u>.* **vs.** *Ils ont <u>copieusement</u> mangé.*

In both Spanish and French, there is a pattern for making adverbs from adjectives. The suffix *-mente/-ment* is added to the feminine (or neutral, if there is no gender contrast) singular form of the adjective. This process is extremely productive and is limited only by the plausibility of the derived adverb.

*copiosa* → *copiosamente*/*copieuse* → *copieusement*
*libre* → *libremente*/*libre* → *librement*

There are a few additional details in French. The masculine form of the adjective is used as the base if it ends in a vowel, *absolu* → *absolument*, or in *-ent* or *-ant* (with the orthographic adjustment of *-nt* to *-mm*), *constant* → *constamment*. There are also a number of exceptions, for example, *brièvement*, *gentiment*, *énormément*.

### Detalles/Détails

In Spanish, if several derived adverbs are used together, the suffix is attached only to the last: *Me gustaría adelgazar fácil y eficazmente*. This does not happen in French: *Je voudrais maigrir facilement et efficacement*.

French and Spanish have many nonderived adverbs in common: *antes/ avant*, *ayer/hier*, *mañana/demain*, *hoy/aujourd'hui*, etc. The meanings of the adverbs that are not cognates is often hard to guess and must be learned as vocabulary.

*a menudo ~ fréquemment*
*a veces ~ parfois*
*además ~ en plus*
*ahora ~ maintenant*
*antiguamente ~ autrefois, jadis*
*aun ~ même*
*bastante ~ assez*
*cerca ~ près*
*demasiado ~ trop*
*en adelante ~ désormais*
*entonces, luego ~ alors, ensuite, puis, donc*
*lejos ~ loin*
*muy ~ très*
*primero ~ d'abord*
*pronto ~ bientôt*
*quizá(s), tal vez ~ peut-être*
*rápidamente ~ vite* (**French also has** *rapidement*)
*siempre ~ toujours*
*también ~ aussi*
*temprano ~ de bonne heure, tôt*
*todavía, aún ~ encore*

With regard to adverb position, adverbs that follow the verb go after the entire verb in Spanish *(Han comido copiosamente)* but follow only the conjugated part of the verb in French *(Ils ont copieusement mangé)*.

## 6B. PREPOSITIONS

Comparar/Comparer
*Gracias <u>por</u> los chocolates.* **vs.** *Merci <u>pour</u> les chocolats.*

Even for languages as closely related as French and Spanish, words that appear to be the same in the two languages may not have the same meaning. This is especially true in the case of prepositions, which are words that name relationships. Though prepositions are very high-frequency words, there are just a handful of them, which means that each one must have a meaning broad enough to apply to a wide range of relationships. These meanings are so broad, in fact, that no preposition in one language maps perfectly onto a preposition in another.

Consider the following examples. If you know how *por* is used in Spanish, it looks as if Spanish is consistent while French is unpredictable.

*por ahora ~ pour l'instant*
*por lo menos ~ au moins*
*por fin ~ enfin*
*por ejemplo ~ par exemple*

But, starting with French *en* and going to Spanish gives the opposite impression.

*en avant ~ hacia adelante*
*en effet ~ en efecto*
*en fait ~ de hecho*
*en bas ~ abajo*

What these examples show is this: the overlap between cognate prepositions in the two languages is not perfect. Sometimes the overlap is quite large: *a ~ à, con ~ avec, contra ~ contre, entre ~ entre, según ~ selon, sin ~ sans*. But, though the overlap between Spanish *a* and French *à*, for example, is large, it is not perfect.

*un molinillo de café ~ un moulin à café*

All relationships have to be given a prepositional name, that is, they have to be assigned to one of the broad prepositional categories, and the logic of this assignment may be different for the two languages. For all of these reasons, it is often best to treat prepositional phrases as idioms.

When prepositions are followed by a pronoun, the pronoun will be from the list of disjunctive pronouns, that is, those that can be stressed. These are Spanish *mí*, *ti*, *él/ella/Ud./sí*, *nosotros*, *(vosotros)*, *ellos/ellas/ Uds./sí* and French *moi*, *toi*, *lui/elle/soi*, *nous*, *vous*, *eux/elles/soi*. With the preposition *con*, Spanish has the forms *conmigo*, *contigo*, and *consigo (avec moi, toi, soi)* rather than *\*con mí/ti/sí*.

### *Por/para* and *pour/par*

*Por* and *pour* have a common origin (Latin *pro*), as do *para* and *par* (Latin *per*). *Para* is actually a compound preposition to which *a* has been added, and—just as the preposition *a* in Spanish introduces the goal of motion—*para* introduces a physical, temporal, or metaphorical goal. Here, the uses of *pour* overlap with those of *para*.

**destination:** *Salió para Madrid. ~ Il est parti pour Madrid.*
**recipient:** *El mensaje es para ti. ~ Le message est pour toi.*
**beneficiary:** *Los voluntarios trabajan para los pobres. ~ Les volontaires travaillent pour les pauvres.*
**deadline:** *La versión final es para el lunes. ~ La version finale est pour lundi.*
**purpose:** *Es un remedio para la tos. ~ C'est un remède pour la toux.*
**intention:** *Te doy el libro para que lo leas. ~ Je te donne le livre pour que tu le lises.*

*Por*, in contrast, introduces a source of motion. The goal vs. source contrast is consistently expressed by *para* vs. *por* in Spanish and often by *pour* vs. *par* in French.

*Está fabricado para Carrefour. ~ Il est fait pour Carrefour.*
   vs. *Está fabricado por Carrefour. ~ Il est fait par Carrefour.*
*Es muy alto para un francés. ~ Il est très grand pour un Français.*
   vs. *Es muy alto por ser/porque es noruego. ~ Il est très grand parce qu'il est norvégien.*

Other uses of these prepositions, however, diverge. For example, in French, gratitude is seen as flowing toward the object of the preposition, resulting in *merci pour*. In Spanish, in contrast, the object of the preposition is the cause of gratitude, resulting in *gracias por*.

## Detalles/Détails

The French preposition *chez* comes from Latin *casa*. Spanish has the word *casa*, but not the preposition. A prepositional phrase composed of *chez* + a noun referring to people or a personal pronoun (*chez moi*, etc.) is equivalent to Spanish *en casa de X* or, in the spoken language, *donde X: Vamos a comer donde David.* ~ *On va manger chez David. Chez*, however, can be used less literally, as in *chez Balzac (en la obra de Balzac)*.

### 6.1 Ejercicio/Exercice

Here are some sentences containing verb + preposition combinations in which the prepositions differ in French and Spanish. Match the sentences and observe the prepositions.

| | |
|---|---|
| Contamos <u>con</u> guías profesionales. | Il s'inquiète <u>au</u> sujet du prix. |
| Sueño <u>con</u> una playa caribeña. | Votre seule tâche consiste <u>à</u> vous détendre. |
| Se preocupa <u>por</u> el precio. | Je rêve <u>d'</u>une plage des Caraïbes. |
| Nos acercamos <u>a</u> la fecha límite. | Nous comptons <u>sur</u> des guides professionnels. |
| Su única tarea consiste <u>en</u> relajarse. | Nous nous approchons <u>de</u> la date limite. |

## *De* and *en* in French

In both French and Spanish, *de/de* is the PARTITIVE preposition, which means that it links a part to a whole. "Whole" can be understood metaphorically as source, origin, and composition.

*El avión salió de Londres a las 3.* ~ *L'avion est sorti de Londres à trois heures.*
*Esta especia es de México.* ~ *Cette épice est du Mexique.*
*Es una mesa de madera.* ~ *C'est une table de bois.*

French and Spanish do not always express the part/whole relationship in the same way. Look at the French question below, where *du vin* means *some wine*, that is, part of all the wine there is. In Spanish a bare noun (a noun without any article) has partitive meaning.

*Tu veux du vin?* ~ *¿Quieres vino?*

In the answer to this question, *en* stands for the prepositional phrase *du vin* (*en* is called a pronoun, but is really a pro-prepositional phrase). In Spanish, the bare noun need not be replaced by anything at all.

*J'en ai, merci.* ~ *Ya tengo, gracias.*

*En* regularly replaces prepositional phrases beginning with *de* in French; in Spanish, no replacement is needed.

*Qui s'occupe du dîner?* ~ *¿Quién se ocupa de la cena?*
*Je m'en occupe.* ~ *Me ocupo yo.*

*En* stands for part of a whole even when the preposition *de* is not present.

*J'ai deux yaourts. Tu en veux un [des deux]?* ~ *Tengo dos yogures.*
 *¿Quieres uno?*

### 6.2 Ejercicio/Exercice

Answer each of the French questions below using *en* in place of the prepositional phrase. *En* should be placed just before the verb.

*Tu n'as pas envie de ça? (¿No tienes ganas de eso?) Si . . .*
*Avez-vous besoin de sel? (¿Necesita sal?) Oui . . .*
*Est-ce que vous prenez du sucre? (¿Toma azúcar?) Oui . . .*
*Combien de morceaux voulez-vous? (¿Cuántos trozos quiere?) Je . . .*

## Detalles/Détails

The preposition *de* is sometimes dropped in contemporary Spanish. For example, it has become so normal to say *antes/después que (avant/ depuis que)* rather than standard *antes/después de que* that the version without *de* now appears even in writing. And, because speakers are criticized for these missing prepositions, there is a corresponding tendency to add *de* where it doesn't belong: *pensar de que (penser que)* instead of standard *pensar que*.

## *Y* in French

Like *en*, *y* replaces prepositional phrases. But *y* is LOCATIVE rather than partitive; it replaces prepositional phrases introduced by *à*, *en*, *dans*, *sur*, *sous*, *derrière*, and other prepositions referring to the location of things—but not people. (Nouns referring to people after the preposition *à* are classified as indirect objects.) It has no equivalent in Spanish—though it is the historical source of the final *-y* of the verb *hay (il y a)*.

*Tu vas au restaurant?* ~ *¿Vas al restaurante?*
*Oui, j'y vais.* ~ *Sí, voy.*

*Y* also appears with verbs that are accompanied by these prepositions, such as *goûter à*.

*Est-ce que vous avez goûté au vin?* ~ *¿Ha probado el vino?*
*Non, je n'y ai pas goûté.* ~ *No, no lo he probado.*

---

### 6.3 Ejercicio/Exercice

Match these common French expressions containing locative *y* with the corresponding expressions in Spanish. (And notice that the word *y* exists in Spanish—with a completely different meaning.)

| | |
|---|---|
| *Allons-y.* | *No hay de qué.* |
| *Il n'y a pas de quoi.* | *Ya está.* |
| *Pensez-y.* | *Vamos a llegar/a lograrlo.* |

| | |
|---|---|
| *J'y suis et j'y reste.* | *Vámonos.* |
| *On va y arriver.* | *Piense en ello.* |
| *Ça y est.* | *Aquí estoy y aquí me quedo.* |

## 6C. COGNATES AND FALSE COGNATES

French and Spanish share many, many words inherited from Latin. For the most part, this is an advantage. Occasionally, however, changes in usage have resulted in false cognates: words whose apparent similarity is misleading. Long lists of false cognates give the impression that these words are a real problem, but the problem disappears once the false correspondence is recognized.

---

**6.4 Ejercicio/Exercice**

The underlined words in the sentences on the left might tempt you into using a false cognate in the corresponding sentences on the right. What words belong in the blanks?

| | |
|---|---|
| Mis _padres_ nos _esperan_ para comer. | Mes _____ nous _____ pour manger. |
| Tengo que _quitar_ la _mancha_ del _mantel_. | Je dois _____ la _____ de la _____. |
| Cette tranche qui _reste_ est trop _large_ pour moi. | El trozo que _____ es demasiado _____ para mí. |
| Le chef est _fier_ de son _succès_. | El cocinero es _____ de su _____. |

---

Some genuine cognate words are hard to identify because changes in pronunciation—as recorded in spelling—have masked their common origin. Knowing about changes that occurred in one language, but not the other, can reveal the cognates.

When stressed, the Latin short vowels *ĕ* and *ŏ* regularly became the diphthongs *ie* and *ue* in Spanish. As a result, there are cognates that have a diphthong in Spanish but a simple vowel in French. Many Spanish/French cognates follow the pattern below:

*ciento ~ cent*      *bueno ~ bon*
*diente ~ dent*      *cuenta ~ compte*
*fiesta ~ fête*       *fuera ~ hors*
*siete ~ sept*       *muerte ~ mort*
*tiempo ~ temps*   *puente ~ pont*

**6.5** Ejercicio/Exercice

There are diphthong/simple vowel alternations between related words in the vocabulary of Spanish because the diphthongization occurred only in stressed syllables. Identify the stressed syllable in each of the words below and observe where the diphthongs *ie* and *ue* appear. (The same diphthong/simple vowel contrast appears in the verb system of Spanish, as discussed in the verb charts.)

*ciento/centenar*    *bueno/bondad*
*diente/dental*      *cuenta/contable*
*fiesta/festival*     *fuera/forastero*
*siete/setenta*      *muerte/mortal*
*tiempo/temporal*  *puente/pontón*

**6.6** Ejercicio/Exercice

The French words below once had an *s* in them, which came after the vowel marked with the symbol ^. The Spanish cognates still have the *s* in them. Knowing this, can you predict what the Spanish words are?

*bête*
*côte*
*être*
*fête*

*île*

*maître*

*même*

*pâte*

**6.7** Ejercicio/Exercice

As French developed from Latin, syllable-final *l* before a consonant often turned into the vowel *u*. In Spanish, the *l* is still present. Can you predict what the cognates of these French and Spanish words are?

*aube*

*haut*

*faux*

*faute*

*palma*

*saltar*

*salvaje*

*salvar*

## 6D. LOANWORDS

Both Spanish and French have some words dating from pre-Roman times, Spanish from Iberian and Basque, and French from Celtic. The French counting system, for example, in which the numbers from eighty to ninety-nine are based on *quatre-vingts* (four multiplied by twenty), is from Celtic, though the words themselves are from Latin. The pre-Latin component, though, is very small compared to the number of words borrowed from more recent contacts.

### Borrowing from Arabic
The vocabulary of Spanish contains thousands of words borrowed from Arabic. This is not surprising, as speakers of Arabic occupied parts of the Iberian Peninsula from 711 (the first Moorish invasion) until 1492 (the reconquest of Granada). The words themselves reveal what

things—foods, household items, concepts—Europe needed to borrow names for. Many Arabisms were borrowed into French as well, often via Spanish.

*ajedrez* ~ *échecs*
*alcachofa* ~ *artichaut*
*alcaparra* ~ *câpre*
*álgebra* ~ *algèbre*
*algodón* ~ *coton*
*almizcle* ~ *musc*
*azafrán* ~ *safran*
*arroz* ~ *riz*
*azúcar* ~ *sucre*
*berenjena* ~ *aubergine*
*cenit* ~ *zénith*
*cero* ~ *zéro*
*jarabe* ~ *sirop*
*naranja* ~ *orange*

The *a-* or *al-* at the beginning of many of these words comes from the article in Arabic, which was misunderstood as part of the noun in the borrowing process.

**6.8** Ejercicio/Exercice

Many Arabic words made their way into English via French. Look at the list of Arabisms above and identify the English borrowings.

In France, the old Arabic borrowings are supplemented by current borrowings from Arabic-speaking citizens of France. As always, most of the borrowed words are nouns, the names of borrowed things. Among these new words are *couscous, hammam, henné, kebab,* and *khôl (cuscús/cuzcuz, hammam, henna, kebab, kohl)*. There are also many slang words borrowed from Arabic, a few of which have passed into general use: *chouïa, flouze, maboul, toubib (poquito, dinero, loco, médico)*.

**Borrowing from the Americas**
Spanish has borrowed words from the indigenous languages of the Americas, the result of colonization. Subsequent borrowing from Spanish into French reveals, again, that the items in question did not exist in Europe.

**6.9** Ejercicio/Exercice

Can you guess which language these words were borrowed from? Assign each to its original language: Nahuatl (central Mexico), Quechua (Andean region), or Taino/Arawak (Caribbean).

*aguacate* ~ *avocat*
*cacahuete* ~ *cacahouète*
*cacao* ~ *cacao*
*chocolate* ~ *chocolat*
*huracán* ~ *ouragan*
*maíz* ~ *maïs*
*pampa* ~ *pampa*
*papa/patata* ~ *patate*
*quinina* ~ *quinine*
*tabaco* ~ *tabac*
*tomate* ~ *tomate*

There are many indigenous languages still spoken in the Americas, and some of these language families—Quechua, Maya, Guarani, and Aymara—have millions of speakers. Indigenous languages continue to be sources of borrowing for Spanish, though many of the borrowings are limited in scope to the region where a given language is spoken.

**Borrowing from English**
French and Spanish have been borrowing from English for centuries, but the pace of borrowing has increased since the Second World War.

**6.10** Ejercicio/Exercice

The words below are borrowings from English which are old enough to have been respelled with Spanish orthography. In French, the original spelling has been retained, but the spelling does not mean that the borrowings are pronounced as in English. Predict how these words will be pronounced in French and then listen to them.

*champú* ~ *shampooing*
*cóctel* ~ *cocktail*
*estándar* ~ *standard*
*estrés/estresar* ~ *stress/stresser*
*hamburguesa* ~ *hamburger*
*líder* ~ *leader*
*nócaut* ~ *K-O*
*sándwich/sánduche/sánguche* ~ *sandwich*
*tenis* ~ *tennis*
*yanqui* ~ *yankee*

**Mutual borrowing**
Of course, French and Spanish contribute words to one another. Because of geographic proximity, European Spanish borrows some words from French that American Spanish borrows from English. For example, the word for *computer* in Spain is the masculine *ordenador* (from French *ordinateur*), while the word in most of Latin America is the feminine *computadora* (from English *computer*).

**6.11** Ejercicio/Exercice

Here are some French words borrowed from Spanish. Predict how they will sound in French and then listen to them.

*aficionado*
*cafétéria*
*corrida*

*enchilada*
*fajita*
*guerrilla*
*macho*
*patio*
*poncho*
*rodéo*
*tapas*

 **6.12** Ejercicio/Exercice

Here are some Spanish words borrowed from French. Where does stress fall in all of these words? Most Spanish words are stressed on the next-to-last syllable, so how can the stress pattern of these borrowings be explained?

*bulevar*
*camión*
*carné/carnet*
*chofer*
*coñac*
*jardín*
*marrón*
*pantalón*
*plató*
*tupé*

## 6E. DERIVED WORDS

French and Spanish have a renewable linguistic resource that creates new words by adding prefixes and suffixes to root words. Knowing how this process works in one language is good preparation for understanding and creating derived words in the other language.

### 6.13 Ejercicio/Exercice

Here are some Spanish words made with the suffix -*azo*. When this suffix is added to a noun X, the result is a word meaning "a blow with X." Can you guess the meaning of these derived words?

*batazo*—from English *baseball bat*
*cabezazo*—from *cabeza (tête)*
*codazo*—from *codo (coude)*
*cuartelazo*—from *cuartel (caserne)*
*manotazo*—from *mano (main)*
*payazo*—from English *pie*
*plumazo*—from *pluma (plume)*
*portazo*—from *puerta (porte)*

### 6.14 Ejercicio/Exercice

Here are some French words made with the suffix -*ard*. When this suffix is added to a noun X, the result is a word meaning "someone associated with/from X," often with a negative connotation. Can you guess the meaning of these derived words?

*banlieusard*—from *banlieue (cercanías)*
*soixante-huitard*—from 1968
*campagnard*—from *campagne (campo)*
*fêtard*—from *fête (fiesta)*
*motard*—from *moto (moto)*
*routard*—from *route (ruta)*
*sorbonnard*—from *l'Université de Paris-Sorbonne*
*zonard*—from *zone (barrio bajo)*

**Suggestions for further practice**
1. Choose a parallel text from this book (or find one online, a good source is albalearning.com) and highlight all of the French/Spanish cognates that you find.

2. An excellent way to increase your active vocabulary is to read in French or Spanish about your hobbies and, if possible, engage in them with native speakers (such as by playing online games). Keep a list of useful terms, especially verbal constructions such as, for chess: *faire échec et mat au roi adverse ~ poner en jaque mate al rey adversario.*

## Chapter 7

# ¿CUÁL ES LA LENGUA MÁS DIFÍCIL?
# QUELLE LANGUE EST LA
# PLUS DIFFICILE?

When people use the words *hard* or *easy* to describe a language, they usually mean "different from or similar to my language." All human languages are complex, but different aspects of a language may be more or less complex relative to other languages. There is no language that is maximally complex in every possible way; if there were, the speakers of that "hard" language would have to be more intelligent than those of every other language. Rather, languages are relatively complex or simple in different ways.

If asked which language—French or Spanish—is more difficult, many speakers of English would choose French. If that is your choice, you will be surprised to know that French speakers who have studied Spanish often say that Spanish is a hard language.

In fact, what is difficult about any new language depends on the language(s) that you already know.

FOR SPEAKERS OF SPANISH, FRENCH IS "HARD" BECAUSE:
- There are more contrastive sounds, both vowels and consonants. This creates two challenges for the learner: to recognize new contrasts and to make the sounds that create those contrasts.
- There are more contrastive sounds than there are letters in the alphabet to spell them. And there are words that have retained an antiquated spelling that no longer corresponds to pronunciation. So, spelling is complicated and learning to spell is a long process—as French-speaking school children will attest.

- All written languages differ from their respective spoken languages, but the gap between writing and speaking in French is particularly wide. Many grammatical distinctions (e.g., gender and number on nouns and adjectives, person and number on verbs) are inaudible and have to be learned visually.
- The gap between formal and informal French is also very wide, and it affects all aspects of the language. Where liaison occurs between words, for example, varies depending on degree of formality. Even basic functions like asking a question or expressing negation involve issues of formality/informality. In order to read French, you have to learn to decode sentence structures that you may not have heard; in order to write correct French, you have to learn to produce these structures.
- The pronouns *y* and *en* (and the frequent expression of the partitive with the preposition *de*) do not exist in Spanish, so they may seem superfluous, and the justification and the contexts for their use have to be learned.
- There are two auxiliary verbs used to form the compound tenses, *être* and *avoir*, where Spanish has only *haber*.

FOR SPEAKERS OF FRENCH, SPANISH IS "HARD" BECAUSE:
- Stress is contrastive, so attention must be paid to where words are stressed in addition to individual sounds.
- Articles always show the gender of nouns; that is, there is no neutralization of gender as in French in the plural articles and the shortened article *l'*, so you must know the gender of nouns in order to use them correctly.
- There are more verb forms in the subjunctive, and there are more contexts in which there is a choice between indicative and subjunctive. There are even two forms of the past subjunctive (though the form ending in *-se* is slowly disappearing in most dialects).
- There are more forms of address—and their corresponding verbs. In Latin America, there are three options: singular *tú/vos* vs. *usted*, and plural *ustedes*. In some dialects *tú* and *vos* are in competition, so both forms must be learned, though most of the corresponding verb forms are the same. In Spain there are four options: singular

*tú* vs. *usted*, and plural *vosotros* vs. *ustedes*, though *vosotros* is much more frequently used than *ustedes*.

- Verb-subject order is common in subordinate clauses, so it may be necessary to use multiple cues, including the personal *a*, to identify the subject.

- There are two verbs corresponding to French *être*, *ser* and *estar*, and the difference between them must be learned.

- There is no single country that exercises the same influence in the Hispanophone world that France does in the Francophone world. With more than 350 million speakers, Latin America is important not just demographically, but economically and culturally as well. Latin American varieties of Spanish are different from those of Spain and also from one another, and regional features have to be learned.

# ANSWER KEY

## CHAPTER 1

**1.1**
*Argelia (ar ge lia)*
*Brasil (bra sil)*
*Canadá (ca na da)*
*Corea (co re a)*
*España (es pa ña)*
*Japón (ja pon)*
*México (me xi co)*
*Perú (pe ru)*

## CHAPTER 2

**2.1**
*La semana pasada la Asamblea General llamó la atención del Consejo de Seguridad hacia una situación política susceptible de poner en peligro la seguridad internacional.*

**2.2**
*la cooperación económica ~ la coopération économique*
*la organización internacional ~ l'organisation internationale*
*el tratamiento desigual ~ le traitement inégal*
*el mecanismo institucional ~ le mécanisme institutionnel*

**2.3**
*la ley → las leyes*            *las resoluciones → la resolución*
*la agencia → las agencias*     *las agendas → la agenda*
*el voto → los votos*           *los países → el país*
*el presidente → los presidentes*  *los miembros → el miembro*

**2.4**
*la loi → les lois*             *les résolutions → la résolution*
*l'agence → les agences*        *les agendas → l'agenda*
*le vote → les votes*           *les pays → le pays*
*le président → les présidents*  *les membres → le membre*

**2.5**

*Cet* accord entre *nos* pays est essentiel. ~ *Este* acuerdo entre *nuestros* países es esencial.

*Les ambassadeurs ont apposé* *leur* signature sur *ces* documents. ~ *Los embaja-dores han puesto* *su* firma en *estos* documentos.

*Elle a posé* *sa* question à *ce* candidat-*ci*. ~ *Ella le hizo* *su* pregunta a *este* candidato.

*Notre* politique extérieure n'admet pas *cette* possibilité-*là*. ~ *Nuestra* política exterior no admite *esa* posibilidad.

## CHAPTER 3

**3.1**

No subject pronouns are needed in Spanish.

**3.2**

*¿La has visto?*

*¿Los has visto?*

*¿Lo has visto?*

*¿Las has visto?*

**3.3**

| | | |
|---|---|---|
| A: | *¡A mí me parece absurda esta novela!* | *Ce roman me paraît absurde!* |
| B: | *A mí también. Me da dolor de cabeza.* | *A moi aussi, ça me donne mal à la tête.* |
| A: | *¿Por qué nos la recomendó la profe, entonces?* | *Alors, pourquoi est-ce que la prof nous l'a recommandé?* |
| B: | *Porque al autor le dieron el Nobel.* | *Parce qu'on a donné le Nobel à l'auteur.* |
| A: | *¡Qué cínico eres!* | *Tu es vraiment cynique, toi!* |

**3.4**

| | | |
|---|---|---|
| P: | *¿Ya lo hiciste?* | *Tu l'as fait?* |
| E: | *No, porque no lo entiendo.* | *Non, parce que je ne le comprends pas.* |
| P: | *Te lo voy a explicar/Voy a explicártelo.* | *Je vais te l'expliquer.* |
| E: | *Lo puedo entender/Puedo enten-derlo hasta aquí.* | *Je peux le comprendre jusque-là.* |
| P: | *Tienes que hacerlo así.* | *Tu dois le faire comme ça.* |
| E: | *¡Ah! Ahora déjeme terminarlo solo.* | *Ah! Maintenant laissez-moi le finir tout seul.* |

## 3.5

La section *que* tu veux est pleine.

Les étudiants *qui* ont fini peuvent partir.

C'est le film *qu'*on a vu en classe.

J'ai une question *qui* est assez courte.

C'est l'étudiante *qui* vient d'entrer.

## 3.6

Ça ne fait rien. ~ No pasa nada.

Ça suffit. ~ Basta.

Ça fait longtemps. ~ Hace tiempo.

Ça vaut la peine. ~ Vale la pena.

Ça m'est égal. ~ Me es igual.

Ça se voit. ~ Se ve.

Ça dépend. ~ Depende.

## 3.7

C'est qui? ~ ¿Quién es?

C'est moi. ~ Soy yo.

C'était nécessaire. ~ Era necesario.

C'est la même chose. ~ Es lo mismo.

C'est mieux. ~ Es mejor.

C'est vrai. ~ Es verdad.

C'est dommage. ~ Es una lástima.

## CHAPTER 4

### 4.3

Les spectateurs ont *suivi* la finale (no agreement, m. sg.).

L'équipe allemande est *devenue* championne du monde (f. sg.).

Deux cent mille Argentins sont *venus* (m. pl.).

Beaucoup de personnes se sont *rassemblées* (f. pl.).

### 4.4

Je *suis* tombée amoureuse du football quand *j'ai* assisté avec mon père au match d'ouverture du Mondial en 1998. Nous *sommes* arrivés très tôt et il m'*a* acheté un maillot officiel de l'équipe de France que *j'ai* tout de suite mis.

### 4.7

Gracias por la invitación a ese magnífico partido. Espero que *pudieras* descansar al día siguiente. Es probable que *vuelva* en el otoño. Te llamaré cuando *estén* finalizados mis planes.

**4.8**

**Cause-effect:**

*Si nada arriesgas, nada tendrás.* ~ *Si tu ne risques rien, tu n'auras rien.*

*Si dices las verdades, pierdes las amistades.* ~ *Si on dit la vérité, on perd l'amitié.*

**Contrary-to-fact:**

*Si la mar fuera vino, todo el mundo sería marino.* ~ *Si la mer était du vin, tout le monde serait marin.*

*Si Dios no existiera, habría que inventarlo.* ~ *Si Dieu n'existait pas, il faudrait l'inventer.*

**4.9**

*Je <u>suis</u> un monstre d'intelligence. soy*

*Vous regrettez d'<u>être</u> intelligent? ser*

*Ce <u>sont</u> des gens qui ont un très grand sens pratique. son*

*Je ne <u>suis</u> jamais seul. estoy*

*J'ai l'habitude d'<u>être</u> toujours avec Salvador Dali. estar*

# CHAPTER 5

**5.1**

*¿Dónde está (usted)?* or *¿Dónde estás?*

*Estoy en el aeropuerto.*

*Où êtes-vous?/Où est-ce que vous êtes?* or *Où es-tu?/Où est-ce que tu es?*

*Je suis à l'aéroport.*

*¿Cuándo sale?*

*Sale mañana.*

*Quand part-elle?* or *Quand est-ce qu'elle part?*

*Elle part demain.*

*¿Tiene el pasaporte?* or *¿Tienes/tenés el pasaporte?*

*Sí, lo tengo.*

*Avez-vous le passeport?/Est-ce que vous avez le passeport?* or *As-tu le passe-port?/Est-ce que tu as le passeport?*

*Oui, je l'ai.*

*¿Viajan con los niños?*

*No, no viajan con ellos.*

*Voyagent-ils avec les enfants?* or *Est-ce qu'ils voyagent avec les enfants?*

*Non, ils ne voyagent pas avec eux.*

**5.2**

*Ça marche pas.* ~ *No funciona.*

*C'est pas vrai/possible/nécessaire.* ~ *No es verdad/posible/necesario.*

*Ça fait rien.* ~ *No pasa nada.*

*J'en peux plus.* ~ *No puedo más.*
*J'ai pas le choix.* ~ *No tengo otra opción.*
*J'ai aucune idée.* ~ *No tengo (ninguna) idea.*
*Il y en a plus.* ~ *No hay más.*
*On a plus rien à dire.* ~ *No tenemos nada más que decir.*

**5.3**
*No me lo digas.* ~ *Ne me le dis pas.*
*Vete.* ~ *Va-t'en.*
*No te preocupes.* ~ *Ne t'inquiète pas.*
*Díselo.* ~ *Dis-le-lui/leur.*
*Explícamelo.* ~ *Explique-le-moi.*
*No les hables de eso.* ~ *Ne leur en parle pas.*

**5.4**
*Conocí a tu **encantadora** vecina en el barco.* ~ *J'ai rencontré ta **charmante** voisine sur le bateau.*
*Prefiero los viajes **organizados**.* ~ *Je préfère les voyages **organisés**.*
*En París puedes ver la **famosa** Mona Lisa.* ~ *A Paris tu peux voir la **célèbre** Joconde.*
*¿Cuánto es la tarifa **normal**?* ~ *Quel est le tarif **normal**?*
*Vamos a esquiar en la **magnífica** cordillera de los Andes.* ~ *On va skier dans la **magnifique** Cordillère des Andes.*
*Pasaremos tres días en **histórico** Edimburgo.* ~ *Nous allons passer trois jours dans l'**historique** ville d'Édimbourg.*

## CHAPTER 6

**6.1**

| | |
|---|---|
| *Contamos con guías profesionales.* | *Nous comptons sur des guides professionnels.* |
| *Sueño con una playa caribeña.* | *Je rêve d'une plage des Caraïbes.* |
| *Se preocupa por el precio.* | *Il s'inquiète au sujet du prix.* |
| *Nos acercamos a la fecha límite.* | *Nous nous approchons de la date limite.* |
| *Su única tarea consiste en relajarse.* | *Votre seule tâche consiste à vous détendre.* |

**6.2**
*Si, j'en ai envie.*
*Oui, j'en ai besoin/nous en avons besoin.*
*Oui, j'en prends/nous en prenons.*
*J'en veux/nous en voulons un (deux, trois . . . ).*

**6.3**

*Allons-y.* ~ *Vámonos.*

*Il n'y a pas de quoi.* ~ *No hay de qué.*

*Pensez-y.* ~ *Piense en ello.*

*J'y suis et j'y reste.* ~ *Aquí estoy y aquí me quedo.*

*On va y arriver.* ~ *Vamos a llegar/a lograrlo.*

*Ça y est.* ~ *Ya está.*

**6.4**

*padres* ~ *parents* (not *pères* in this context); *esperan* ~ *attendent* (not *espèrent* in this context)

*quitar* ~ *enlever* (not *quitter* ~ *dejar/salir*); *manche* ~ *tache* (not *manche* ~ *manga*); *mantel* ~ *nappe* (not *manteau* ~ *abrigo*)

*reste* ~ *queda* (not *resta* ~ *soustrait*); *large* ~ *grande/ancho* (not *largo* ~ *long*)

*fier* ~ *orgulloso* (not *fiero* ~ *féroce*); *succès* ~ *éxito* (not *suceso* ~ *événement*)

**6.5**

| | |
|---|---|
| *cien*to/cente*nar* | *bue*no/bon*dad* |
| *dien*te/den*tal* | *cuen*ta/con*table* |
| *fies*ta/festi*val* | *fue*ra/foras*tero* |
| *sie*te/se*ten*ta | *muer*te/mor*tal* |
| *tiem*po/tempo*ral* | *puen*te/pon*tón* |

**6.6**

*bête* ~ *bestia*

*côte* ~ *costa*

*être* ~ *estar*

*fête* ~ *fiesta*

*île* ~ *isla*

*maître* ~ *maestro*

*même* ~ *mismo*

*pâte* ~ *pasta*

**6.7**

*aube* ~ *alba*

*haut* ~ *alto*

*faux* ~ *falso*

*faute* ~ *falta*

*palma* ~ *paume (de la main)*

*saltar* ~ *sauter*

*salvaje* ~ *sauvage*

*salvar* ~ *sauver*

**6.8**

chess/checkers, artichoke, caper, algebra, cotton, musk, saffron, rice, sugar, aubergine, zenith, zero, syrup, orange

**6.9**

Nahuatl: *aguacate, cacahuete, cacao, chocolate, tomate*; Quechua: *pampa, papa/ patata, quinina*; Taino/Arawak: *huracán, maíz, tabaco*

**6.12**

The stress falls on the last syllable in all of the words because they are borrowed from French, and in French the stress is always on the last syllable of individual words.

**6.13**

hit in baseball, butt with the head, elbow in the ribs, military coup (*golpe* in Spanish), slap, pie in the face, stroke of the pen, slam of a door

**6.14**

suburbanite, participant in the May 1968 protests in France, peasant, partier, biker, backpacker (and a popular tourist guide), Sorbonne student, someone from a poor neighborhood

# PARALLEL TEXTS

## EL PASTOR MENTIROSO

*Había una vez un joven pastor que tenía muchas ovejas. A veces el pastorcito se aburría de estar[1] solo en el campo y un día, para divertirse, gritó, "¡El lobo, el lobo!" Al escuchar esto, los campesinos se dijeron "¡Vamos!, y corrieron a prestarle ayuda. Pero al llegar encontraron al[2] pastorcito riéndose de ellos. "¡Ja, ja, ja! Los engañé."*

*Otro día, el pastorcito volvió a gritar, "¡El lobo, el lobo!" Otra vez acudieron los campesinos y otra vez vieron que el pastorcito se burlaba de ellos.*

*Inevitablemente, llegó el día en que realmente apareció el lobo. "¡El lobo!" gritó el pastorcito. "¡Se lo juro, es el lobo! ¡Vengan rápido!" Pero esta vez los campesinos no hicieron nada, y el lobo destrozó todo el rebaño.*

*La moraleja de la historia es, Al[3] mentiroso nunca se le cree, aunque diga[4] la verdad.*

Notice:

1. The copula *estar* is used with adjectives when the adjective names a state (not a characteristic).
2. *A* (combined here with the article *el*) precedes human, specific direct objects.
3. *A* (combined here with the article *el*) precedes human, specific direct objects.
4. The subjunctive (of the verb *decir*) is used after *aunque* when the following information is presented as unimportant or irrelevant.

## LE BERGER MENTEUR

*Il était une fois un jeune berger qui avait beaucoup de moutons.[1] Des fois le petit berger s'ennuyait de rester seul à la campagne et un jour, pour s'amuser, il cria "Au loup, au loup!" Entendant cela les paysans se dirent "Allons-y!" et coururent lui apporter de[2] l'aide. Mais en arrivant ils trouvèrent le petit berger se riant d'eux. "Ha, ha, ha! Je vous ai trompés[3]."*

*Un autre jour, le petit berger recommença à crier, "Au loup, au loup!" Encore une fois les paysans lui vinrent en aide, et encore une fois virent que le petit pasteur se moquait d'eux.*

*Inévitablement arriva le jour où le loup apparut pour de vrai. "Au loup" cria le petit pasteur. "Je le jure, c'est le loup. Venez vite!" Mais cette fois-ci[4] les paysans ne firent rien, et le loup détruisit tout le troupeau.*

*La morale de l'histoire est, On ne croit jamais le menteur, même s'il dit la vérité.*

Notice:
1. The preposition *de* has partitive meaning.
2. The preposition *de* has partitive meaning.
3. Though the story is told in the simple past, spoken dialogue is in the compound past. And, the participle agrees in number with the preceding direct object *les*.
4. The demonstrative adjective has two parts, one before the noun and one after.

MUNDIAL 2014

*Ha ganado el mejor equipo[1]. Alemania marcó un gol durante la segunda pró-*
*rroga, consiguiendo en Río su cuarta Copa del Mundo. El equipo alemán llegó a*
*campeón del mundo venciendo, tal como lo hizo en 1990 en Italia, a[2] la Argentina*
*por 1 a 0. Esta vez, el joven Mario Götze, 22 años, dio el golpe decisivo en el minuto*
*113. Lionel Messi, capitán del equipo de Argentina, tiró un pénalti en el minuto*
*122, pero el milagro no llegó a producirse. A pesar de la derrota, Messi fue elegido*
*mejor jugador del Mundial 2014.*

*Dos cientos mil argentinos llenaron el estadio del Maracaná, venidos de Bue-*
*nos Aires y de la Pampa a pie, en auto, en moto y en autobús, y el resto de la*
*población del país vecino vio el partido en casa. En Alemania, 35 millones de*
*espectadores siguieron la final delante de su televisor, y otros tantos millones en*
*los bares y restaurantes o delante de pantallas gigantes, al aire libre. Dos días más*
*tarde, se reunieron decenas de miles de personas[3] para acoger en Berlín al[4] equipo*
*nacional, que ha conseguido[5] para Alemania su primer título mundial después*
*de la reunificación del país en 1990.*

Notice:
1. The subject follows the verb, as often happens in Spanish when the subject is the most informative part of the sentence.
2. *A* precedes a personified direct object.
3. Verb-subject order
4. *A* (combined here with the article *el*) precedes human, specific direct
   objects.
5. Here and in the first sentence of the text, the Spanish present perfect
   corresponds to the French compound past when the action of the verb
   has continuing relevance in the present.

MONDIAL 2014

*La meilleure équipe[1] a gagné. L'Allemagne a marqué un but dans la seconde prolongation, remportant à Rio sa quatrième Coupe du monde. L'équipe allemande[1] est devenue[2] championne du monde vainquant, comme ce fut[3] le cas en 1990 en Italie, l'Argentine par 1 à 0. Cette fois, le jeune Mario Götze, 22 ans, a donné le coup de grâce à la 113e minute. Lionel Messi, capitaine de l'équipe d'Argentine, a tiré un coup franc à la 122e minute, mais le miracle n'a pas eu lieu. Malgré la défaite, Messi a été élu meilleur joueur du Mondial 2014.*

*Deux cent mille Argentins ont rempli le stade Maracana, venus de Buenos Aires et de la Pampa à pied, en voiture, à moto ou en bus, et tout le reste de la population du pays voisin a vu le match chez lui. En Allemagne, 35 millions de spectateurs ont suivi la finale devant leur téléviseur, et d'autres millions dans les bars et restaurants ou devant des écrans géants, en plein air. Deux jours plus tard, des dizaines de milliers de personnes se sont rassemblées[4] pour accueillir à Berlin l'équipe nationale, qui a rapporté à l'Allemagne son premier titre mondial depuis la réunification du pays en 1990.*

Notice:

1. The noun *équipe* is feminine in French, as revealed by the feminine adjective. Cognate *equipo* is masculine in Spanish.
2. After *être* the participle agrees with the subject in gender and number, like any adjective.
3. The rest of the text is in the compound past, often used in articles about popular subjects such as sports and entertainment. The use of the simple past here signals another, more distant, past time.
4. Participle agreement after *être*.

## ENTREVISTA AL PINTOR SALVADOR DALÍ (1971)

*Salvador Dalí, ¿'cómo se define?*

SD: *Soy uno de los raros artistas contemporáneos que siempre han rehusado pertenecer a un partido o una agrupación política cualquiera.*

*¿Usted² mismo, se considera inteligente?*

SD: *Soy un monstruo de inteligencia.*

*¿Lamenta ser inteligente?*

SD: *Lo lamento por mi pintura.*

*¿Está por la honestidad en la pintura?*

SD: *Por la honestidad en todo.*

*¿Se³ puede ser surrealista sin saberlo?*

SD: *Sobre todo sin saberlo.*

*¿Qué piensa de quienes coleccionan sus cuadros?*

SD: *Son personas que tienen un enorme sentido práctico.*

*¿A su entender, ¿sirve para algo un museo?*

SD: *Es uno de los medios más seguros de aumentar mi fortuna y la de mi país.*

*¿Todavía tiene grandes enemigos vivos?*

SD: *Creo que ninguno. Pero querría que el mundo entero fuese⁴ mi enemigo.*

*El placer, la fiesta, ¿qué papel desempeñan en su vida?*

SD: *Un papel esencial. Creo que la vida debe ser una fiesta continua.*

*¿Cómo soporta la soledad?*

SD: *Nunca estoy solo. Tengo la costumbre de estar siempre con Salvador Dalí. Créame, eso es una fiesta permanente.*

Notice:

1. Questions are marked orthographically both at the beginning and the end.
2. The subject pronoun *usted* is used here because of the modifying *mismo*; there is no subject pronoun in any of the other sentences.
3. *Se* used in place of a specific subject is the most common option for impersonal and passive sentences in Spanish.
4. The conditional in the main clause is followed by the past subjunctive in the subordinate clause (which could also be *fuera*, the *-ra* form of the past subjunctive).

## INTERVIEW AVEC LE PEINTRE SALVADOR DALI (1971)

*Salvador Dali, comment vous¹ définissez-vous?*

SD: *Je suis un des rares artistes contemporains qui aient toujours refusé d'appartenir à un parti ou à un groupement politique quel qu'il soit.*

*Vous-même, vous vous trouvez intelligent?*

SD: *Je suis un monstre d'intelligence.*

*Vous regrettez d'être intelligent?*

SD: *Je le regrette pour ma peinture.*

*Vous êtes pour l'honnêteté en peinture?*

SD: *Pour l'honnêteté en tout.*

*On² peut être surréaliste sans le savoir?*

SD: *Surtout sans le savoir.*

*Que pensez-vous des gens qui collectionnent vos tableaux?*

SD: *Ce sont des gens qui ont un très grand sens pratique.*

*A votre avis, ça sert à quoi, un musée?*

SD: *C'est l'un des moyens les plus sûrs d'augmenter ma fortune et celle de mon pays.*

*Avez-vous encore de³ grands ennemis vivants?*

SD: *Aucun, je crois. Mais je voudrais que le monde entier soit⁴ mon ennemi.*

*Le plaisir, la fête, quel rôle jouent-ils dans votre vie?*

SD: *Un rôle essentiel. Je crois que la vie doit être une fête continuelle.*

*Comment supportez-vous la solitude?*

SD: *Je ne suis jamais seul. J'ai l'habitude d'être toujours avec Salvador Dali. Cela, croyez-moi, c'est une fête permanente.*

Notice:

1. Here, and throughout, the subject pronoun appears with conjugated verbs.
2. *On* used in place of a specific subject is the most common option for impersonal and passive sentences in French.
3. The conditional in the main clause is followed by the present subjunctive in the subordinate clause.
4. Modern spoken French would have *des* here.

Source: "Salvador Dali va plus loin avec L'Express," *L'Express* (Paris), March 1, 1971.
Translation: "Entrevista a Salvador Dalí," *Panorama* (Buenos Aires), April 6, 1971.

# VERB CONJUGATION CHARTS

## SPANISH VERBS

You can see the full conjugation of model Spanish verbs in the dictionary, and of virtually any verb online (enter the infinitive into a search engine). So, the purpose of this chart is not to list all possible variations and exceptions, but to explain important patterns.

Verbs are listed, in the dictionary and online, in the infinitive form: *-ar, -er, -ir.* The *-ar* verbs comprise the largest, and most regular, class. The *-er* and *-ir* verbs are so similar that you need to take note of where they differ from one another.

The orthography of Spanish verb forms is quite regular; most of the adjustments involve the spelling of the last consonant in the stem before certain endings. You can find a complete list by entering "orthographic-changing verbs in Spanish" into a search engine.

Forms are listed below in the order *yo, tú/vos, él/ella/usted, nosotros/nosotras, (vosotros/vosotras), ellos/ellas/ustedes.* The use of *tú, vos,* and *vosotros* (in parentheses because it is used only in Spain) is discussed in chapter 3H.

### Simple Forms
*Present indicative, regular verbs*
*-ar*: add the endings *-o, -as/ás, -a, -amos, (-áis), -an* to the capitalized stem

*HABLar: hablo, hablas/hablás, habla, hablamos, (habláis), hablan*

*-er*: add the endings *-o, -es/-és, -e, -emos, (-éis), -en*

*COMer: como, comes/comés, come, comemos, (coméis), comen*

*-ir*: add the endings *-o, -es/-is, -e, -imos, (-ís), -en* (only *nosotros* and *vos/vosotros* forms differ from *-er* verbs)

*VIVir: vivo, vives/vivís, vive, vivimos, (vivís), viven*

*Present indicative, stem-changing verbs*
Stem-changing verbs have two stems: one containing *e* or *o* when the stem is unstressed (as in the infinitive), and one containing the diphthongs *ie* and *ue* in stressed syllables.

In addition to the model verbs below, common *e/ie* stem-changing verbs include *cerrar, comenzar, empezar, negar, entender, convertir, mentir.*

PENS*ar: pienso, piensas/pensás, piensa, pensamos, (pensáis), piensan*
PERD*er: pierdo, pierdes/perdés, pierde, perdemos, (perdéis), pierden*
PREFER*ir: prefiero, prefieres/preferís, prefiere, preferimos, (preferís), prefieren*

In addition to the model verbs below, common *o/ue* stem-changing verbs include *encontrar, mostrar, probar, recordar, soñar, mover, volver, morir.*

CONT*ar: cuento, cuentas/contás, cuenta, contamos, (contáis), cuentan*
POD*er: puedo, puedes/podés, puede, podemos, (podéis), pueden*
DORM*ir: duermo, duermes/dormís, duerme, dormimos, (dormís), duermen*

In a few *-ir* stem-changing verbs, the unstressed and stressed stems contain *e* and *i*, respectively. Common *e/i* stem-changing verbs include *decir, repetir, seguir, servir.*

PED*ir: pido, pides/pedís, pide, pedimos, (pedís), piden*

*Present indicative, verbs with consonant variations in the* yo *form*
These common verbs have consonants in the *yo* form that do not appear in the infinitive. The first group has /g/ inserted between the stem and the -o. Some of these verbs, marked with *, are also stem-changing (except for the *yo* form). In addition to the verb below, other verbs that show this pattern are *poner, salir, *venir.*

*TEN*er: tengo, tienes/tenés, tiene, tenemos, (tenéis), tienen*

Two high-frequency verbs, *hacer* and *decir*, exhibit a variation that involves substituting /g/ for the *-c-* of the infinitive.

HAC*er: hago, haces/hacés, hace, hacemos, (hacéis), hacen*
*DEC*ir: digo, dices/decís, dice, decimos, (decís), dicen*

A third pattern involves inserting /ig/ after the stem. The verb *traer* also shows this pattern.

CA*er: caigo, caes/caés, cae, caemos, (caéis), caen*

A fourth pattern involves inserting /k/ after the final consonant of the stem. The inserted consonant is spelled *c* and the (now) preceding consonant *z*. Other verbs of this group are *crecer, establecer, traducir*.

*CONOCer: conozco, conoces/conocés, conoce, conocemos, (conocéis), conocen*

Finally, four verbs, *dar, estar, ir,* and *ser,* have *yo* forms that end in -*y* in the present indicative: *doy, estoy, voy,* and *soy*.

*Imperfect indicative, regular verbs*
The imperfect is almost perfectly regular. Only three verbs are irregular in the imperfect: *ir, ser,* and *ver* (and *ver* is irregular only in having the stem *VE-*). Note that there is no difference between the *yo* and *él* forms in the imperfect, and -*er* and -*ir* verbs are conjugated exactly the same.

-*ar*: add the endings -*aba, -abas, -aba, -ábamos, (-abais), -aban*

*HABLar: hablaba, hablabas, hablaba, hablábamos, (hablabais), hablaban*

-*er* and -*ir*: add the endings -*ía, -ías, -ía, -íamos, (-íais), -ían*

*COMer: comía, comías, comía, comíamos, (comíais), comían*
*VIVir: vivía, vivías, vivía, vivíamos, (vivíais), vivían*

*Preterit indicative, regular verbs*
Some of the preterit endings are distinctive, but two of them require attention. (1) The difference between the ending of the *él* form of the preterit of -*ar* verbs and the ending of the *yo* form of the present is stress: *él habló* vs. *yo hablo*. Stress is contrastive in Spanish, so this difference is not just a matter of spelling. (2) For -*ar* and -*ir* verbs, the *nosotros* form is the same in the present tense and the preterit; context prevents misunderstanding. As in the imperfect, -*er* and -*ir* verbs are conjugated exactly the same. The verb *dar* is conjugated with -*er*/-*ir* endings added to the minimal stem *D-*.

The preterit is the only conjugation in which the *tú/vos* form does not end in -*s*. For this reason, many speakers add a final /s/ in speaking—though this is not accepted in the written language.

-*ar*: add the endings -*é, -aste, -ó, -amos, (-asteis), -aron*

*HABLar: hablé, hablaste, habló, hablamos, (hablasteis), hablaron*

*-er* and *-ir:* add the endings *-í, -iste, -ió, -imos, (-isteis), -ieron*

COMer: *comí, comiste, comió, comimos, (comisteis), comieron*
VIVir: *viví, viviste, vivió, vivimos, (vivisteis), vivieron*

### Preterit indicative, stem-changing *-ir* verbs

Verbs of the *-ir* class that are stem-changing (e.g., *decir, pedir, preferir, repetir, seguir, servir, dormir, morir*) show an *e>i* or *o>u* stem change in the third-person (i.e., *él* and *ellos*) forms of the preterit.

PEDir: *pedí, pediste, pidió, pedimos, (pedís), pidieron*
DORMir: *dormí, dormiste, durmió, dormimos, (dormís), durmieron*

### Preterit indicative, verbs with separate preterit stems

Some common verbs have a different stem in the preterit than in the present. These verbs also share a slightly different set of preterit endings (note that the endings of the *yo* and *él* forms are not stressed, as they are with regular preterit verbs). In addition to *tener*, other verbs with irregular stems in the preterit include *decir (DIJ-), hacer (HIC-), estar (ESTUV-), poder (PUD-), poner (PUS-), querer (QUIS-), saber (SUP-), venir (VIN-).*

Add the endings *-e, -iste, -o, -imos, (-isteis), -ieron* to the preterit stem.

tener (TUV-): *tuve, tuviste, tuvo, tuvimos, (tuvisteis), tuvieron*

### Future indicative

This verb form is easy to remember: it consists of the infinitive plus the present tense forms of the verb *haber*, written without the *h* (in the case of the *vosotros* form, without the first syllable). Historically, the infinitive + *haber* combination was written as two words, which explains why all of the modern endings are stressed.

Add the endings *-é, -ás, -á, -emos, (-éis), -án* to all infinitives.

HABLAR: *hablaré, hablarás, hablará, hablaremos, (hablaréis), hablarán*

A few common verbs have a slightly altered stem in the future tense: *decir (DIR-), haber (HABR-), hacer (HAR-), poner (PONDR-), querer (QUERR-), saber (SABR-), tener (TENDR-), venir (VENDR-).*

*Conditional indicative*

The conditional consists of the infinitive plus the imperfect endings corresponding to the verb *haber*.

Add the endings *-ía, -ías, -ía, -íamos, (-íais), -ían* to all infinitives.

HABLAR: *hablaría, hablarías, hablaría, hablaríamos, (hablaríais), hablarían*

The verbs that have an altered stem in the future tense also have that stem in the conditional.

*Present subjunctive*

The present subjunctive is based on the *yo* form (minus the *-o* ending) of the present indicative. So, whatever that form is, its characteristics will carry over to the present subjunctive. There is one set of endings for *-ar* verbs, containing the "opposite" vowel *e*, and another for *-er* and *-ir* verbs, containing the "opposite" vowel *a*. Note that there is no difference between the *yo* and *él* endings.

Verbs of the *-ar* class with stems ending in *-c, -g* and *-z* are adjusted orthographically before subjunctive endings beginning in *e-*: *toc- + -e = toque*, *lleg- + -e = llegue*, *rez- + -e = rece*. Verbs of the *-er* class with stems ending in *-g* are adjusted orthographically before subjunctive endings beginning in *-a*: *cog- + -a = coja*.

The difference between the ending of the *yo/él* form of the present subjunctive and the ending of the *yo* form of the preterit indicative is stress: *yo/él hable* vs. *yo hablé*. Stress is contrastive in Spanish, so this difference is not just a matter of spelling.

*-ar*: add the endings *-e, -es, -e, -emos, (-éis), -en.*

HABLo: *hable, hables†, hable, hablemos, (habléis), hablen*
PIENSo: *piense, pienses, piense, pensemos, (penséis), piensen*

†There is variation in the *vos* form of the present subjunctive; the forms here are those used in Argentina/Uruguay, where *voseo* is well established.

*-er* and *-ir*: add the endings *-a, -as, -a, -amos, (-áis), -an.*

COMo: *coma, comas, coma, comamos, (comais), coman*
TENGo: *tenga, tengas, tenga, tengamos, (tengáis), tengan*
VIVo: *viva, vivas, viva, vivamos, (viváis), vivan*
PIDo: *pida, pidas, pida, pidamos, (pidáis), pidan*

*Past subjunctive*

The past subjunctive is based on the *ellos* form (minus the *-ron* ending) of the preterit indicative. So, whatever that form is, its characteristics will carry over to the past subjunctive. The same endings are used with all verbs, and a written accent is added to the *nosotros* form to show that stress falls on the stem. Note that there is no difference between the *yo* and *él* endings.

There are two sets of endings in the past subjunctive: one containing *-ra* and one containing *-se*. The *-ra* endings are the most common; the *-se* endings can be learned for recognition.

Add the endings *-ra/-se, -ras/-ses, -ra/-se, -ramos/-semos, (-rais/-seis), -ran/-ses* to all base forms.

*HABLAron: hablara/hablase, hablaras/hablases, hablara/hablase, habláramos/ hablásemos, (hablarais/hablaseis), hablaran/hablasen*

*PIDIEron: pidiera/pidiese, pidieras/pidieses, pidiera/pidiese, pidiéramos/pidié- semos, (pidierais/pidieseis), pidieran/pidiesen*

*TUVIEron: tuviera/tuviese, tuvieras/tuvieses, tuviera/tuviese, tuviéramos/ tuviésemos, (tuvierais/tuvieseis), tuvieran/tuviesen*

## Compound Forms

Spanish has several compound verbs, made by combining forms of the verbs *estar, haber, ir,* and *ser* with the infinitive, participle, and the gerund. These high-frequency verbs have many irregular forms, which appear below; forms that are regular are not listed. Note that *ir* and *ser* share the same forms in the preterit; context prevents misunderstanding.

*ESTAR*
Present: *estoy, estás, está, estamos, (estáis), están*
Preterit: *estuve, estuviste, estuvo, estuvimos, (estuvisteis), estuvieron*
Present subjunctive: *esté, estés, esté, estemos, (estéis), estén*
Past subjunctive: *estuviera/estuviese, estuvieras/estuvieses, estuviera/estuviese, estuviéramos/estuviésemos, (estuvierais/estuvieseis), estuvieran/estuviesen*
*HABER*
Present: *he, has, ha/hay[†], hemos, (habéis), han [†]il y a*
Future: *habré, habrás, habrá, habremos, (habréis), habrán*
Conditional: *habría, habrías, habría, habríamos, (habríais), habrían*
Past subjunctive: *hubiera, hubieras, hubiera, hubiéramos, (hubierais), hubiera*
*IR*
Present: *voy, vas, va, vamos, (vais), van*
Imperfect: *iba, ibas, iba, íbamos, (ibais), iban*

Preterit: *fui, fuiste, fue, fuimos, (fuisteis), fueron*
Present subjunctive: *vaya, vayas, vaya, vayamos, (vayáis), vayan*
Past subjunctive: *fuera/fuese, fueras/fueses, fuera/fuese, fuéramos/fuésemos, (fuerais/fueses), fueran/fuesen*

SER
Present: *soy, eres/sos, es, somos, (sois), son*
Imperfect: *era, eras, era, éramos, (erais), eran*
Preterit: *fui, fuiste, fue, fuimos, (fuisteis), fueron*
Present Subjunctive: *sea, seas, sea, seamos, (seáis), sean*
Past subjunctive: *fuera/fuese, fueras/fueses, fuera/fuese, fuéramos/fuésemos, (fuerais/fueses), fueran/fuesen*

## Perfect forms

To form the present, past, future, and conditional perfect, the present, imperfect, future, and conditional of *haber* can be combined with the participle of any verb. (The preterit of *haber* + participle is a possible combination, but is rarely used.) Regular participles are formed by adding *-ado* to the stem of *-ar* verbs, and *-ido* to the stem of *-er* and *-ir* verbs. Some common verbs have irregular participles: *abrir (abierto), decir (dicho), escribir (escrito), hacer (hecho), morir (muerto), poner (puesto), romper (roto), ver (visto), volver (vuelto).*

## Progressive forms

To form the present, past, future, and conditional progressive, the present, imperfect or preterit, future, and conditional of *estar* can be combined with the gerund of any verb. Regular gerunds are formed by adding *-ando* to the stem of *-ar* verbs, and *-iendo* to the stem of *-er* and *-ir* verbs. Stem-changing *-ir* verbs that have *e > i* or *o > u* in the third person forms of the preterit, also have this change in the gerund, for example, *viniendo (venir)*.

## Compound future/conditional forms

To form the *going-to* future or conditional, the present or imperfect of *ir* is combined with the infinitive.

## Passive voice

There are several passive voice options in Spanish. One of them—now more common in writing than in speaking—is a combination of *ser* + participle.

## Command Forms

With the exception of the affirmative commands for *tú* and *vos*, all command forms come from the subjunctive (see above). Regular command forms for *tú* have the same form as the *tú* form of the present indicative, minus the *-s* ending: *habla, come, vive.* Some common verbs have monosyllabic command forms: *di (decir), haz (hacer), pon (poner), sal (salir), sé (ser), ten (tener), ve (ir).*

The affirmative *vos* commands are accented on the final syllable and can be derived by removing the *-r* from the infinitive: *hablá, comé, viví.* This derivation produces regular *vos* commands for all verbs: *decí, hacé, poné, salí, sé, tené.* In the case of *ir*, the *vos* command comes from the verb *andar: andá* (because removing the *-r* from *ir* leaves almost nothing).

### FRENCH VERBS

You can see the full conjugation of model French verbs in the dictionary, and of virtually any verb online (enter the infinitive into a search engine). So, the purpose of these charts is not to list all possible variations, but to explain important patterns.

Verbs are listed, in the dictionary and online, in the infinitive (*-er, -ir, -re*) form; it is important to recognize, however, that the verb stem cannot always be identified by removing these endings from the infinitive. The *-er* verbs comprise the largest, and most regular, class.

Forms are listed below in the order *je, tu, il/elle, nous, vous, ils/elles.* The subject pronoun *on*, used both as an impersonal subject and as a substitute for *nous*, is conjugated in the third person singular (like *il/elle*).

Verb forms in French show orthographic adjustments such as (*g/ge*) and (*c/ç*) in verbs like *manger* and *commencer*; (*i/y*) in verbs like *voir* and *essayer*; (*e/è or é/è*) in verbs like *lever, acheter, céder*, and *répéter*; and (*t/tt and l/ll*) in verbs like *jeter* and *appeler*. Such orthographic adjustments can easily be looked up and will not be covered completely below.

### Simple Forms
#### Present indicative
The present indicative has by far the greatest variation in conjugation patterns of all the tenses in French, but much of the variation is orthographic. The following regularities apply, however: *je* forms end in *-e* or *-s*; *tu* forms end in *-s*; *il/elle* forms end in *-e, -t* or null (no added ending); *nous* forms end in *-ons*; *vous* forms end in *-ez*; and *ils/elles* forms end in *-ent.* The only exceptions occur in the five highest-frequency verbs: *être, avoir, aller, faire, dire.*

The present tense of all verbs—except for highly irregular *aller, avoir*, and *être*—is characterized by homophony of the *je, tu*, and *il/elle* forms; in speaking, only subject pronouns (and liaison, if it occurs) serve to distinguish one from another. In the *-er* group, and in some verbs of the other two groups, the homophony of the *je, tu*, and *il/elle* forms extends to the *ils/elles* form.

The present indicative is the base form for a number of other verb forms: the imperfect and gerunds (*nous* stems), the present subjunctive (*nous* and *ils* stems), and the command forms (*tu*, *nous*, and *vous* forms).

### Present indicative, -er verbs (89% of all verbs)

The present indicative of this largest group of verbs is highly regular. Four of the forms have the same pronunciation and two of the forms, *nous* and *vous*, are distinctive because the endings add a syllable to the stem.

Add the endings *-e, -es, -e, -ons, -ez, -ent* to the capitalized stem:

*PARLer: je parle, tu parles, il/elle parle, nous parlons, vous parlez, ils/elles parlent*

A small number of verbs ending in *-ir* are conjugated like *-er* verbs: *couvrir, cueillir, offrir, ouvrir, souffrir,* and their derivatives (e.g., *accueillir, découvrir*):

*OFFRir: j'offre, tu offres, il/elle offre, nous offrons, vous offrez, ils/elles offrent*

### Present indicative, -ir verbs (7% of verbs)

Almost half of the verbs ending in *-ir* belong to a highly regular group. These two hundred plus verbs have the same endings as all *-ir* verbs (*-s, -s, -t, -ons, -ez, -ent*) but are distinguished by the insertion of the INFIX *-ss-* between the stem and the endings of the *nous*, *vous*, and *ils/elles* forms. Verbs in this group include *agir, choisir, finir, obéir, réussir,* etc., as well as many verbs derived from adjectives such as *grandir, rougir, maigrir.*

Add the endings *-s, -s, -t, -ons, -ez, -ent* to the capitalized stem.

*FINIr: je finis, tu finis, il/elle finit, nous finissons, vous finissez, ils/elles finissent*

The remaining *-ir* verbs are less regular due to a number of orthographic variations and stems. Nevertheless, they fall into recognizable patterns. For example, in the verbs *DORMir, MENTir, PARTir, SENTir, SERVir, SORTir* (and their derivatives) the final consonant of the stem drops out of the singular forms before a consonant ending: for example, *dorm + -s = dors, sent + -t = sent.*

*DORMir: je dors, tu dors, il/elle dort, nous dormons, vous dormez, ils/elles dorment*

The remaining -*ir* verbs that do not follow these two patterns can be looked up and are not listed here.

*Present indicative, -re verbs (4% of all verbs)*
This group includes the remaining 4 percent of verbs whose endings are: -*s*, -*s*, -*t* or null ending, -*ons*, -*ez*, -*ent*.

The stem of a majority of -*re* infinitives ends in a consonant, and many of these verbs pattern like the *dormir* group of verbs above (for similar reasons) except that there is a null ending in the *il/elle* form when the stem ends in -*d*. Verbs in this category include *PERDre*, *ROMPre*, *VIVre*, *RENDre*, etc.

*PERDre: je perds, tu perds, il/elle perd, nous perdons, vous perdez, ils/elles perdent*
*ROMPre: je romps, tu romps, il/elle rompt, nous rompons, vous rompez, ils/elles rompent*

The high-frequency verb *PRENDre* (and its derivatives) differs from this pattern in the *nous*, *vous*, and *ils/elles* forms:

*PRENDre: je prends, tu prends, il/elle prend, nous prenons, vous prenez, ils/elles prennent*

The remaining -*re* verbs that do not follow this pattern can be looked up and are not listed here.

*Imperfect indicative*
The imperfect is perfectly regular except for the orthographic adjustments (*g/ge*) and (*c/ç*). It is formed by adding the endings -*ais*, -*ais*, -*ait*, -*ions*, -*iez*, -*aient* to the stem of the present indicative *nous* form. The only exception is the irregular verb *être*, which has the imperfect stem *ÉT-*.

*nous PARLons* (present indicative): *je parlais, tu parlais, il/elle parlait, nous parlions, vous parliez, ils/elles parlaient*
*nous COMMENÇons* (present indicative): *je commençais, tu commençais, il/elle commençait, nous commencions, vous commenciez, ils/elles commençaient*
*nous MANGEons* (present indicative): *je mangeais, tu mangeais, il/elle mangeait, nous mangions, vous mangiez, ils/elles mangeaient*

Note that, barring liaisons, there is no difference in pronunciation between the *je*, *tu*, *il/elle*, and *ils/elles* forms; and the *nous* and *vous* forms are pronounced the same as the present subjunctive.

*Future indicative*
Future (and conditional) stems are the full infinitive of *-er* and *-ir* verbs, and the infinitive of *-re* verbs less the final *-e*. The endings are the present indicative of *avoir* with the *nous* and *vous* forms truncated: *-ai, -as, -a, -ons, -ez, -ont*:

PARLER: *je parlerai, tu parleras, il/elle parlera, nous parlerons, vous parlerez, ils/elles parleront*

Note that orthographic adjustments in the present indicative conjugations of *-er* verbs occur in the future stem, for example, *appeler (APPELLER-), enlever (ENLÈVER-), etc.*

FINIR: *je finirai, tu finiras, il/elle finira, nous finirons, vous finirez, ils/elles finiront*
PRENDRe: *je prendrai, tu prendras, il/elle prendra, nous prendrons, vous prendrez, ils/elles prendront*

A small number of verbs have irregular future/conditional stems. Among the most common are *faire (FER-), devoir (DEVR-), savoir (SAUR-), vouloir (VOUDR-), voir (VERR-), venir (VIENDR-), tenir (TIENDR-), falloir (FAUDR-), avoir,* and *être* (see chart below).

*Conditional*
The conditional is formed from the same stem as the future with the endings of the imperfect: *-ais, -ais, -ait, -ions, -iez,* and *-aient*.

PARLER: *je parlerais, tu parlerais, il/elle parlerait, nous parlerions, vous parleriez, ils/elles parleraient*

*Present subjunctive*
The present subjunctive is highly regular, with the endings *-e, -es, -e, -ions, -iez, -ent*. For almost all verbs, the present subjunctive is based on the common stem of the present indicative *ils* and *nous* forms. Where these two forms diverge, there are two subjunctive stems (see below). Because they share the same stems and endings, the *nous* and *vous* forms are the same in the present subjunctive and the imperfect indicative.

PARLent/PARLons **(present indicative):** *je parle, tu parles, il/elle parle, nous parlions, vous parliez, ils/elles parlent*

For -*er* verbs, the *je, tu, il/elle,* and *ils/elles* forms are the same as the present indicative. In other words, neither these forms nor the *nous* and *vous* forms described above are uniquely subjunctive.

*FINISSent/FINISSons* (present indicative): *je finisse, tu finisses, il/elle finisse, nous finissions, finissiez, ils/elles finissent*

When the *ils* form (the subjunctive stem), has the infix -*ss*-, then the infix appears in all forms of the present subjunctive. Here only the *ils/elles* form is the same as the present indicative.

In the two largest groups of highly regular present-tense conjugations (exemplified above), the stem of *ils* is the same as the stem of *nous*. However, there is a small number of verbs (e.g., *venir, devoir, appeler, lever,* etc.) in which the two stems are stressed and spelled differently. In these verbs, the *nous* stem is used for the *nous* and *vous* forms and the *ils* stem is used for the other four.

*venir*
Stem 1 *VENons* (present indicative): *nous venions, vous veniez*
Stem 2 *VIENNent* (present indicative): *je vienne, tu viennes, il/elle vienne, ils/elles viennent*
*appeler*
Stem 1 *APPELons* (present indicative): *nous appelions, vous appeliez*
Stem 2 *APPELLent* (present indicative): *j'appelle, tu appelles, il/elle appelle, ils/elles appellent*

In addition to *aller, avoir,* and *être* (see below), only seven verbs are irregular in the subjunctive: three with one stem, *faire (FASS-), pouvoir (PUISS-),* and *savoir (SACH-)*; two with two stems, *valoir (VAL-/VAILL-)* and *vouloir (VOUL-/VEUILL-)*; and two impersonal verbs, *falloir (il faille)* and *pleuvoir (il pleuve)*.

## Command Forms
The command forms consist of the *tu, nous,* and *vous* forms of the present indicative, without the subject pronouns. The -*s* ending of the *tu* form of -*er* verbs (including *aller*) is dropped.

*PARLER: parle, parlons, parlez*
*ALLER: va, allons, allez*

Note the -*s* of the *tu* form in -*er* verbs is reinserted before *y* or *en*, for example, *parles-en, vas-y*.

*PARTIR: pars, partons, partez*

There are only four irregular verbs in the imperative and they are formed from the present subjunctive:

*AVOIR: aie, ayons, ayez*
*ÊTRE: sois, soyons, soyez*
*SAVOIR: sache, sachons, sachez*
*VOULOIR: veuille, veuillons, veuillez*

Note that *veuillons* and *veuillez* are formed from the *tu* form, since the present subjunctive *vous* form is *vouliez*.

### Present participle
Present participles are formed from the present indicative *nous* stem and the ending -*ant*:

*APPRENons* (present indicative): *apprenant*
*COMMENÇons* (present indicative): *commençant*

When the present participle follows the preposition *en*, it functions as a gerund:
*En allant au marché, j'ai vu ma cousine.*
   Besides *avoir* and *être* (see chart below) there is only one irregular participle:

*SAVOIR: sachant*

### Compound Forms
Compound verbs in French are formed by combining a conjugated form of the verbs *aller*, *avoir*, and *être* with the infinitive or past participle. These high-frequency verbs have a number of irregular forms which you can see below.

*ALLER* (past participle *allé*; present participle *allant*)
Present indicative: *je vais, tu vas, il/elle va, nous allons, vous allez, ils/elles vont*
Present subjunctive (two stems): *j'aille, tu ailles, il/elle aille, nous allions, vous alliez, ils/elles aillent*
Future/conditional: *j'irai/irais, tu iras/irais, il/elle ira/irait, nous irons/irions, vous irez/iriez, ils/elles iront/iraient*
Imperfect: *j'allais, tu allais, il/elle allait, nous allions, vous alliez, ils/elles allaient*

Simple past: *j'allai, tu allas, il/elle alla, nous allâmes, vous allâtes, ils/elles allèrent*

AVOIR (past participle *eu*; present participle *ayant*)

Present indicative: *j'ai, tu as, il/elle a, nous avons, vous avez, ils/elles ont*

Present subjunctive: *j'aie, tu aies, il/elle ait, nous ayons, vous ayez, ils/elles aient*

Future/conditional: *j'aurai/aurais, tu auras/aurais, il/elle aura/aurait, nous aurons/aurions, vous aurez/auriez, ils/elles auront/auraient*

Imperfect: *j'avais, tu avais, il/elle avait, nous avions, vous aviez, ils/elles avaient*

Simple past: *j'eus, tu eus, il/elle eut, nous eûmes, vous eûtes, ils/elles eurent*

ÊTRE (past participle *été*; present participle *étant*)

Present indicative: *je suis, tu es, il/elle est, nous sommes, vous êtes, ils/elles sont*

Present subjunctive: *je sois, tu sois, il/elle soit, nous soyons, vous soyez, ils/elles soient*

Future/conditional: *je serai/serais, tu seras/serais, il/elle sera/serait, nous serons/serions, vous serez/seriez, ils/elles seront/seraient*

Imperfect: *j'étais, tu étais, il/elle était, nous étions, vous étiez, ils/elles étaient*

Simple past: *je fus, tu fus, il/elle fut, nous fûmes, vous fûtes, ils/elles furent*

*Compound future (futur proche)*

The *going-to* future is formed by combining the present tense of *aller* with an infinitive.

*PARLER: je vais parler*

When transposed to a past time frame, the imperfect of *aller* is used: *j'allais parler*.

*Compound past (passé composé)*

This compound tense is formed by combining *avoir* or *être* with the past participle (see below). Almost all verbs in French combine with *avoir*. The only exceptions are reflexive verbs and the following intransitive verbs, which combine with *être*: *aller, arriver, (re)devenir, (re)naître, mourir, (re)partir, rester, (re)tomber, (re)venir* (and *descendre, entrer, monter, passer, rentrer, retourner, sortir* when used intransitively). When *être* is used as the auxiliary in any compound tense, the past participle agrees in almost all cases with the subject in gender and number. The only exception occurs in reflexive verbs when the reflexive pronoun functions as an indirect object, for example, *ils se sont écrit*.

## Past participles

### -ER VERBS

Past participles of all *-er* verbs are formed by adding *-é* to the infinitive stem:

*PARLER: parlé, APPELER: appelé, ESPÉRER: espéré*

### -IR VERBS

The past participle of the largest class of *-ir* verbs, those conjugated like *finir*, is formed by dropping the *-r*: *FINIR: fini*. The verbs conjugated like *dormir* are also conjugated this way: *DORMIR: dormi*.

There are several other possible endings for the few remaining *-ir* verbs: *-u*, as in *venir (venu), vouloir (voulu)*; *-ert/-ort*, as in *ouvrir (ouvert), mourir (mort)*; and *-is*, as in *asseoir (assis), conquérir (conquis)*.

### -RE VERBS

Like their present indicative conjugations, *-re* verbs have several patterns for forming the past participle, making them hard to predict. However, the past participle of the largest group of *-re* verbs, those conjugated like *perdre*, is formed by dropping *-re* from the infinitive and adding *-u*: *PERDre: perdu*. The participle of a number of other *-re* verbs also ends in *-u*, for example, *lire (lu), plaire (plu), boire (bu), résoudre (résolu)*, etc.

There are several other possible endings for the remaining *-re* verbs: *-is*, as in *mettre (mis), prendre (pris)*; *-t*, as in *dire (dit), faire (fait), craindre (craint)*; *-i*, as in *rire (ri), suivre (suivi)*; and *-é*, as in *naître (né)*.

## Other perfect conjugations

The past perfect (*plus-que-parfait*), future perfect (*futur antérieur*), and conditional perfect are formed by combining the imperfect, future, or conditional, respectively, of the auxiliaries *avoir* or *être* with the past participle.

## Past subjunctive

The past subjunctive is formed by combining the present subjunctive of the auxiliary *avoir* or *être* with the past participle:

*PARLER: j'aie parlé . . . ARRIVER: je sois arrivée . . . SE LAVER: je me sois lavé(e) . . .*

## Compound Participle

The compound participle is formed by combining the present participle of *avoir* or *être* and the past participle of a verb:

*PARLER: ayant parlé*
*VENIR: étant venu(e)(s)*
*SE RÉVEILLER:* reflexive pronoun + *étant réveillé(e)(s)*

**Literary Forms**
*Simple past (passé simple)*
*-er verbs add -ai, -as, -a, -âmes, -âtes, -èrent to the infinitive stem:*

*AIMER: j'aimai, tu aimas, il/elle aima, nous aimâmes, vous aimâtes, ils/elles aimèrent*

Most *-ir* and *-re* verbs are formed by adding *-is, -is, -it, -îmes, -îtes, -irent* to the infinitive stem:

*FINir: je finis, tu finis, il finit, nous finîmes, vous finîtes, ils/elles finirent*

Note that the singular conjugations of *finir* are the same as the present indicative.

*PERDre: je perdis, tu perdis, il perdit, nous perdîmes, vous perdîtes, ils/elles perdirent*

In many irregular verbs, *-u* takes the place of *-i*:

*VOULoir: je voulus, tu voulus, il/elle voulut, nous voulûmes, vous voulûtes, ils/elles voulurent*

Consult a dictionary or verb book to find full conjugations of the *passé simple* (and the *imparfait du subjonctif,* the other simple literary tense).

*Compound literary tenses*
Consult a dictionary or verb book to find full conjugations of the compound literary tenses (e.g., *passé antérieur, plus-que-parfait du subjonctif,* etc.).

# GLOSSARY

(The chapter where words are discussed is in parentheses.)

**approximant (1)** consonant produced when organs of articulation come close to one another without producing friction

**aspect (4)** a category of verbal meaning that encodes how actions/events/situations are perceived in time

**auxiliary (4)** the conjugated part of a compound verb

**clitic (3)** a pronoun that does not take stress and is used in combination with a verb

**cognates (2)** words that share the same original root

**contrary-to-fact (4)** a kind of sentence that refers to a proposition known to be false

**contrastive (1)** the quality that serves to distinguish one word from another

**copula (4)** a verb with minimal meaning that is used to link two parts of a sentence

**digraph (1)** two letters representing one sound

**diphthong (1)** two vowels pronounced in one syllable

**disjunctive (3)** the quality of pronouns that can be stressed and/or used alone

**elision (2)** the loss of a sound or letter when one word appears adjacent to another

**fricative (1)** consonant produced when organs of articulation come so close to one another that air flow produces friction

**gender (2)** the grammatical category that distinguishes masculine from feminine nouns, adjectives, and pronouns in French and Spanish

**gerund/present participle (4)** the impersonal (i.e., without person/number endings) verb form used in Spanish to form the progressive

**infinitive (4)** the impersonal (i.e., without person/number endings) verb form that is also the name of a verb

**infix (French verb charts)** a morpheme inserted between other morphemes in a word

**liaison (1)** in French, the pronunciation of a normally silent word-final consonant before a vowel in a following word

**locative (6)**   denoting location/place

**mood (4)**   a category of verbal meaning that encodes evaluation of the relevance of actions/events/situations

**morpheme (2)**   a word or part of a word that carries meaning

**morphology (introduction)**   how words are formed

**neuter (3)**   having neither masculine nor feminine gender

**occlusive (1)**   consonant produced when organs of articulation come into contact with one another and stop air flow

**orthography (1)**   the conventions for spelling a language

**participle/past participle (4)**   the impersonal (i.e., without person/number endings) verb form used to form the perfect tenses

**partitive (6)**   denoting partialness, part of a whole

**phoneme (1)**   a class of sounds that performs a contrastive function in a given language

**pronoun (2)**   a word that replaces or functions as a noun

**suffix (1)**   a morpheme added to the end of a word

**tense (4)**   a category of verbal meaning that encodes where actions/events/ situations are located on the timeline

**triphthong (1)**   three vowels pronounced in one syllable

**voice (4)**   the grammatical expression of the relationship of an agent to a verbal situation

CPSIA information can be obtained
at www.ICGtesting.com
Printed in the USA
BVHW011025141019
560916BV00015B/10/P